ONCE UPON A TRANSCENDENT REALM

James Martinez

WestBow
PRESS
A DIVISION OF THOMAS NELSON

WestBow Press
A Division of Thomas Nelson
1663 Liberty Drive
Bloomington, IN 47403
www.westbowpress.com
1-(866) 928-1240

ISBN: 978-1-4497-6944-4 (sc)
ISBN: 978-1-4497-7924-5 (hc)
ISBN: 978-1-4497-7925-2 (e)
Library of Congress Control Number: 2012918288

Scripture taken from the King James Version of the Bible.

Some Scripture taken from the American King James version of the Holy Bible.

The graphics desinger:
Vaducci Angelico
Angelic Project
Ploy Productions

The Author photo was taken by:
Jared Tennant
JTPics.com

Printed in the United States of America
WestBow Press rev. date:1/2/2013

This book is dedicated to you, God. Thank-you for igniting the spark of creation before time existed, and for allowing every great dream since then to become a reality. To those who have faith and believe with all their hearts that they can move any mountain, I love you. To my two sons, Christopher "Chance" and Christian, I love you with all of my heart, always. Remember that each second of life is a gift and within each moment is a lesson; and while you pay careful attention to the world, know that God pays careful attention to us all.

Table of Contents

Foreward

During my first synchronous encounter with James Martinez, as I mindfully listened to him describe inspiring insights about "our body's own energy, and how that spiritual energy allows for interactions between one another, and with other spiritual and supernatural realms," in that instant, I knew that I was listening to someone who was 'echoing' my own experience of "transcendence".

I later discovered that both James and I share a common passion for inquiry that has led us to study quantum physics in relation to "transcendence". James writes in his chapter titled Love in a Sunset—Transcendence, "I'd noted there were certain particles traveling through space and time in an undetectable way, and the way they moved intrigued me. I found out that neutrinos mysteriously travel (mostly) undetected from our stratosphere to reach earth. The truth of the particles' movement inspired me, and I needed to know how they moved, so I began researching the principal of particle physics and discovered that space and time were truly navigational. Although I did not have the specifics of this truth just yet, simply knowing of the truth allowed for one of my greatest observations—Transcendence."

James elaborates further by writing, "As I thought back to the visions and translucent image perceptions of the people, places, and things I'd seen, I new that if I altered my thoughts and emotions I could change what and who I interacted with within that grand collective area."

As I reflect upon my own experience of "transcendence" beginning at an early age before I had the ability to intellectualize and articulate what had just happened, and thereafter, actively during my 30's pursuant to a life—transforming experience, for me, listening to James was yet another confirmation about the validity of the multi-sensory reality and experiencing states and otherworldly realms of higher consciousness.

Reading "Once Upon A Transcendent Realm" reminded me of the following poem by Samuel Taylor Coleridge, "What If You Slept" — a poem that I invite you to contemplate, if you already haven't.

What if you slept
And what if
In your sleep
You dreamed
And what if
In your dream
You went to heaven
And there plucked a strange and beautiful flower
And what if
When you awoke
You had that flower in your hand
Ah, what then?

A favorite poem that I love to recite every so often by Rumi, a 13th century Persian poet, allows me to reflect upon what he describes as "nonlocal dynamic in his being"; a term used in parapsychological research, where he claims to be in two places simultaneously. From his poem titled Sitting Together, Rumi writes, "The two of us on a bench in Konya, yet amazingly in Khorasan and Iraq as well, friends abiding this form, yet also in another outside of time, you and I." Rumi's poetry very naturally speaks of telepathy, precognition, communion with the dead, remote vision, and travel in the spirit realms. Translator of Rumi's poems, Coleman Barks writes, "Consciousness roams about through time and space, and beyond those. We are not discretely separate in hermetically sealed units. There's overlap, and the scope of our powers has not been fully mapped. It does seem, though, that those powers have not been equally distributed among us." From my experience and from what Coleman Barks confirms, and that is, "We may all have the potential, but not the opportunity, grace, or compassion, to develop them. We are lovers at varying depths. With enlightened beings the appearance of a gathering must be much different than it is for those of us who are not enlightened. For them, other lighted beings may be present, as well as spirit entities, and maybe even our own potential selves." That is to say that some humans have been graced to have one foot in timeless regions and one solidly here.

I appreciate the fact that James is inviting you and me, and all of us to experience a greater understanding into the depths of who and what we are, and Whose we are from the perspective of one's relationship between the Beloved and the lover — between God and self. James takes all of us on an amazing journey into the depths of various dimensions and spheres of our consciousness and our potential realities about "our body's own energy, and how that spiritual energy allows for interactions between one another, and with other spiritual and supernatural realms" as we are graced with the experience of our own "Once Upon A Transcendent Realm", God Willing.

With Heartfelt Love & Appreciation,
Jihan Barakah
Founder
The Global Quantum Shift

"All who believe in God can do anything."

Preface

Even with all I have encountered, I can remember the beginning; I can remember sensing something extraordinary in this amazing world, and feeling in tune and aligned with something beyond my understanding. With my eyes wide open and my eagerness to discover, I set my course on this journey of love and life. I have come close to life and to death in search of the greatest moments of life. I did not understand early on that the path of truth would lead to so many reverent moments of enlightenment.

I did, however, notice peculiar forces at work in my life from a very early age. I experienced my first near death experience at the age of three, and I had an uncanny ability to pull through many close calls, as if destined for something specific. I did not know that each step of my life was a move closer to insights into the supernatural. We all catch momentary glimpses of the supernatural. We all often experience, in differing measures, a sixth sense;

and the knowledge of such supernatural experiences as an intricate part of life was one of the motivating factors of my journey.

I found myself intrigued with the inexplicable aspects of the supernatural—the déjà vu experiences, ESPs (extrasensory perceptions), telepathy, out-of-body experiences, and even sanctifying moments of divinity. I heard and read many awe-inspiring testimonies of people who claimed to have experienced such experiences, in the hopes that perhaps their stories would be detailed enough to give me insights into this phenomenon. It was a wondrous entreaty that seemed to manifest itself within me and grab hold of me and propel me further towards the unknown. I had often wondered why we lacked the ability to describe or define something that seemed such an intricate part of all of our lives. I found that even with those who had experienced similar encounters, there was no detailed description of answers to the questions I sought and what this internal sensation really was.

I began with a search for the connections that we all have to each other. Each lesson I learned yielded greater understanding and insights into phenomena I once considered inexplicable, mythical, or altogether unattainable. Gaining a greater understanding of what it truly means to be otherworldly allowed for revelations into and beyond the boundaries of the mind, body, and spirit.

This is my tale of the search for a connection that we all share and of the observations I made, how they were made, and what that represents for those of us in search of the greatest truth of all. My observations were made over many years with persistence and perseverance in many disciplined fields of significance which include intuition;

energy of the human body and spirit; and distinctions of the spiritual, supernatural, and celestial. I believe the sincere conclusions I formed go beyond what many would consider palpable or obvious.

I had hopes of finding the missing attribute that compelled me and inexplicably manifested itself within every specific interval in my life, and although my findings took more than eight years to express, they were not in vain. I've come to learn that while in every moment of the wondrous existence of life, there is a greater force at work around each of us; it allows us to achieve the sometimes seemingly impossible and miraculous abilities. Thanks to this force, the abilities I have gained have led to my intrinsic perceptions of the essential nature of the highest order of truth.

This book is a detailed description of my experiences, observations of them, and the miraculous power associated with the divine. Some would call me a spiritual man, a clairvoyant or even a theologian. This metaphysical narration was written from that viewpoint, but I consider it to also be the study and scientific view of natural phenomena and the knowledge acquired.[1] I hope it gives you insight into the uniting force I believe we are all destined to experience in our lives.

---

1   Metaphysical: Based on speculative reasoning and unexamined assumptions that have not been logically examined or confirmed by observation

The Beginning

I simply could not yet grasp the magnitude of all that had just taken place. I knew all that I had just experienced was divine and otherworldly, but I just could not comprehend the importance of such an incredible and magnificent truth. I had just transcended space and time with God, the Father of all creation.

I walked to my kitchen and sat down. I felt slightly overwhelmed with the task that was before me. I wondered, briefly, how I was supposed to do it, how would I accomplish the task of writing a book. At the exact moment of that thought, my phone rang and vibrated with a text message. *Keep it simple and direct.* It was from a friend, but realizing the message had been sent to me the instant I thought of how I would complete the task utterly amazed me. I was in awe at how God was speaking directly to me, and that he would do that with a text message sent by a close friend at the very moment I had thought of how I would approach the enormous task before me. I immediately called my friend and asked him,

"Do you know God is working in your life right now?"

He replied, "How did you know?"

I began to tell him what I had just witnessed. Initially he thought I was referring to what had contributed to him sending me the text. He explained how he had noticed a homeless man at the stoplight asking for help. My friend struck up a conversation and before the light had changed, he had invited the homeless man into his truck and the two of them drove away. He helped the man acquire a job, fed him, clothed him, and found him a temporary place to sleep. The homeless man had been praying to God for help the moment before my friend arrived. After that gesture of goodwill toward another man had concluded, my friend arrived home, got on the computer, and decided to share a social media post with me which read *Keep it simple and direct* at the exact moment I had my thought. What an incredible sign! What a truly amazing gift to witness, and to know that it came directly from God Almighty through my friend.

The fact that I have been part of such a miraculous journey of realizations and observations completely amazes me. I had always heard of the mysterious ways that God works and, truthfully, I had hoped to one day better have an inkling of what such a concept might look like. I believe I found that and much more, all thanks to God.

The Narrowest Gate

I can remember when the journey began—I was experiencing peculiar sensations unlike anything I had ever known, a sense of urgency with each thought, and a strong determination to resolve my curiosity. I had awakened! I'd always been in search of moments of beauty and appeal, but until I awoke, I hadn't realized I had seen them with every breath.

One of the earliest sensations I recall came in the form of my need to find something, anything, and everything that seemed to be missing or out of place within my life. The strong sensation was both undeniable and irrefutable, and I could sense that it had become the bounce in my step and the gleam in my eye. I found that there was much beauty in knowing and even in knowing that I didn't know. It was the entire process of obtaining that unknown knowledge that became incredibly appealing to me. I felt my eyes had opened for the first time. My curiosity took precedence over many of my actions, and I found that all of a sudden I was scrutinizing each moment, not yet knowing what I was searching for, yet yearning to do so. The intrigue with every aspect of God's creation grew with each breath. My thoughts ranged from the exquisiteness of particle physics to the majesty and grandeur of the universe, and everything we know and everything we don't know in between.[2] I simply felt a strong feeling of something and everything at the same time. I describe it as feeling compelled to perceive the essence of the enigma.

With that incredible verve, I began to read articles and research papers and books; I even searched online for anything and anyone who could assist me—hoping perhaps someone could possibly shed new light on why I didn't quite know what it was I was searching for, and what it was. I experienced a strong urge to connect, a sensation that once felt could not be denied. I knew that I was in search of truth and understanding, and I needed and felt drawn towards many subjects, especially those pertaining to philosophy, physics, religion, and ancient wisdom.

The connections

It was during my research and study of ancient wisdom that I read of the golden age: an age which claims we were all at one with everything. I was immediately enthralled having already felt mystically connected to my surroundings. I believed my search for the connections to everything had manifested itself. I became an advanced student of observation of myself and of the moment alike.

Searching for the connection to each moment and everything encapsulated within it, I began to notice

---

2 Particle physics: The branch of physics that deals with the study of subatomic particles, particularly the many unstable particles produced in particle accelerators and high-energy collisions

similarities that we all seemingly have in common with each other but often overlook, perhaps from a lack of understanding or properly perceiving them. I noticed we all start life on earth in a very similar manner, beginning from the beginning. We all experience the first moment of conception; we all have our vessels/bodies develop in our mothers' wombs; we all "practice" [breathing liquid] by inhaling and exhaling amniotic fluid there for a short period of time while each one of us develops. I even began to compare our genes down to the chromosome level.

I studied the spread of a yawn from one person to the next. I noticed how we all depart the wondrous existence here on earth in a similar way. I could see the obvious and the hidden immediately; it was that new found focus on life that aided me, and gave me a more complete perspective and everything began to make perfect sense to me, but I needed to understand our connection, and how we all connect.

I found myself becoming more and more intrigued with subjects that seemed to have very little explanation, or subjects that had no information attached to them at all. I became an astute student of everything and felt the need to understand all that I encountered more clearly. My studies of ancient wisdom led me directly to many ancient civilizations—beginning with Africa, the Middle East, and Asia—which in turn led to my inquiries into the different monotheistic religions and their spiritual foundations and practices. I studied many philosophers, ranging from Carl Jung to Emmanuelle Kant; and I studied physics, reading from papers by Albert Einstein on topics like quantum physics, symmetry, particles, and nuclear fission.[3,4,5] I

3   Quantum physics: The branch of physics that uses quantum theory
4   Particles: A unit of matter smaller than the atom or its main components
5   Nuclear fission: The spontaneous or induced splitting of an atomic nucleus into smaller parts, usually accompanied by a significant

studied life and death and the here and yonder, and it was here when I began to understand the narrow path I believed I was destined to be on.

> *"Enter by the narrow gate; for wide is the gate and broad is the way that leads to destruction, and there are many who go in by it."* (MATTHEW 7:14).

Gentle harmony

My study of the golden age led me to research Buddhism, the religion of most Asians and one studied and practiced by many in the East. What intrigued me the most about Buddhism was that its foundations were deeply rooted in spirituality, with the belief that enlightenment can be attained through direct intuition, a belief and universal truth that I subscribe to.[6] It seemed that the more I studied Zen and the Buddhist philosophy, the more I began to understand spiritual alignment and what it meant to truly center oneself; I felt attuned with everything. Buddhist teachings seemingly allowed me to better understand some of the experiences I was beginning to encounter. At that point along my journey I discovered the great feeling of gentle harmony and I began to notice the signs of life—signs that are everywhere and within each of our paths. These signs take place from the first hour of our first day to the last hour of our last day—they help guide us through our lives. The signs may not necessarily come in the form we are typically accustomed to noticing, but when we become aware of them our lives begin to take on new meanings.

---

release of energy
6   Enlightenment: The state attained when the cycle of reincarnation ends and human desire and suffering are transcended

Synchronicity

I've heard of many who, upon realizing synchronicity for the first time, are simultaneously puzzled and elated.[7] I found those signs of synchronicity to come in many forms, generally within our own lifestyles and habits. Some may see them while observing the same occurrence, often daily and repeatedly, around objects and people. Others may witness what may be dismissed as coincidence. For example, one of the first times I noticed one of those signs, I immediately took it for an innuendo and thought it could be a coincidence. I had only recently awoken, and at the time I still believed in coincidences. I noticed that the events which were transpiring were in direct alignment with my thoughts, emotions, and actions; and upon factoring in all other variables such as other people, their paths, space, time, and all of God's creation, I was simply astonished at how perfectly synchronized each moment fit perfectly within my observations of reality and truth. Furthermore, I was in awe with everything which must have had to happen in order for such a moment to even exist. The synchronous signs were revealing to me that each step and each breath we take has a purpose. I contemplated how my fate could have or would have led to another scenario altogether had one of those steps had a twist or a turn and taken me in a different direction. I was humbled by the thoughts which had led to that actual moment of realization.

Because I was driving when the truth of synchronicity dawned upon me, I was immediately thankful for each individual who had contributed to that great instance of truth. I was thankful for those who produce my vehicle, the ones who had created and built it so that I could be driving in it while reaching that moment. I was also thankful for

---

7   Synchronicity: The coincidence of events that seem related, but are not obviously caused one by the other.

the individuals who first discovered its fuel, and then for those who processed it, and then for those who transported it, and then for those who made the fuel available to propel my vehicle forward so that I might have that very moment. I was also thankful for the DJ, and to those at the radio station that played the music that perfectly depicted that exact moment of my life. I thought of how each person involved helped to contribute the possibility for such a moment or realization to even exist, and I was thankful to them all for how perfectly intertwined it was with my emotional state and physical actions. This very moment is what led to the absolute and undeniable acknowledgement that such signs of synchronicity not only exist, but also that coincidence and accidents don't.

Those types of synchronous signs and observations line the paths on which we walk. They are here and there, and somewhere and somehow placed to faithfully assist us and guide us to where we are all destined to be, and sometimes to also warn us all of where we shouldn't be. If you truly open your eyes and follow your heart, you too may begin to recognize them. Those types of synchronous signs are a part of every day for everyone. Each of our abilities to recognize those supernatural signs is a gift to be embraced, and I've found those signs are a special part of all life.

Auras

It seemed that not only had my apparent sixth sense revealed itself in an intrinsic way, but it had also given way to even more internal abilities I did not yet fully understand. The first time I saw a person's aura was a breathtakingly beautiful experience. I had read about auras before, but I had not yet visually experienced one firsthand. One evening while I experienced a truly joyous moment I noticed a woman who stood before me with an alluring smile on her face, and I could instantly see that her heart was pure. She had an elating presence and a warm feeling all about her. As we conversed she seemed to magically manifest a liveliness which gave way to several brightly florescent and greenish-yellow spheres that rotated several inches above her head. The spheres were less than three centimeters in diameter and moved in a circular and clockwise direction. Ever since then, I could visibly recognize other people's auras at a glance.

Often when I noticed a person's aura it seemed to depict and reveal his/her emotional state of being. If his/her mood is happy and content, then he/she will radiate a light-green aura. If his/her mood is sad, angry, or dissatisfied, his/her aura would be darkened (like a dark brown or even black in some instances). I knew then that there were other internal forces at work all around us. I believe that we all possess the ability to see these extensions of energy we all release and send forth; we simply need to learn to recognize those attributes and practice seeing a person more completely and with more emotion.

Empathic connections

Another of these internal abilities that came forth with great sensitivity was empathy.[8] I began to directly identify with others' emotional feelings as if I were experiencing their sensations for myself. Not only did I begin to identify with others' emotions; I seemed to experience a form of empathy that crossed over space and time and allowed me to directly feel their emotions. It began for me by simply thinking of another person and of his/her well-being until I would actually begin to sense their emotions. This

8   Empathy: The ability to identify with and understand somebody else's feelings or difficulties

11

would generally happen with strong focus and through meditation. I researched and found many instances when twins, both identical and fraternal, had shared an inherent empathic connection to one another. I was intrigued with this new found sensitivity and I wondered how far these empathic connections went. I needed to better understand what I was sensing and why this was happening.

At that point, I realized my new found abilities had become more difficult to conceal. I noticed distinctly that as I became aware of my abilities, something else, something otherworldly had become aware simultaneously. Perhaps what was truly happening was that I simply noticed something that had been here all the while, something that had been preordained long ago but was only now comprehendible at my new level of understanding.

"While we do not look at the things which are seen, but at the things which are not seen. For the things which are seen are temporary, but the things which are not seen are eternal" (2 CORINTHIANS 4:18).

As my studies grew with even more curiosity in regards to our connections to one another, the results began to yield findings that were unraveling truths and overcoming obstacles that I once identified with the mystical, the occult, and the supernatural. I seemed to be changing and adapting to the universe around me. I noticed I had become more ambidextrous—writing, eating, and leading with both my left and right hands. I could sense my range of movement increasing. It seemed my extrasensory perceptions were growing without bounds.

Thoughts

I began to observe the communications we have with one another more closely. I realized there are literally hundreds of languages within the world and they are all based off the power of words, so I began studying words and their meanings in greater depth. I studied semantics and noticed speech patterns I'd not heard before in conversations even across different languages. I could compare it to listening repetitively to a recording of an audio segment on any media player—and instantly having the ability to fast forward, rewind, or replay; and be able to hear the subtle, yet distinctive, underlying thoughts that were previously unrecognizable. I'd seen and heard of instances of subliminal messages (in videos and in recordings of interviews and musical recordings), and now here I was with an ability that seemed very similar to this. I could see that I was beginning to identify and connect with others in a whole new and very unique way. It was then that I realized that the path and those incredible blessings were just the beginning of what the journey would ultimately become.

I was beginning to interpret what was truly on people's foremost thoughts through a simple meeting and conversation. Again, I could tell that that was just the beginning. As my self-awareness developed into a finely tuned extension of my being, I noticed other external forces at work—forces that surround us every day. I observed that when people clear their thoughts and open their hearts and their minds, and I mentally posed a question, the people addressed would generally answer with a slight nod or a shake of their heads. Sometimes they would even respond verbally. I noticed that that phenomenon was even capable of generating insights through and over recorded video.

Understand first that I believe one has to reach a certain state of mind and has to be completely in alignment with everything for an observation such as that to become recognizable. That empirical observation, however, fit perfectly within the synchronous harmony of my life; again, another insightful perspective of God's perfect timing that includes our emotions, thoughts, actions, and conversations with each other.[9] I was astounded at synchronicity's grand yet simple eloquence when I factored in free will, other people's paths and the interwoven complexities of space and time. I could see it was a truth which had always been present all the while, but only at that time was it becoming an intricate part of my life, now that I was awake and able to comprehend such a truth on that new level.

Breathing

While growing more and more into awareness of self, I continued my search for more knowledge and insights into these experiences. I began to study mantra breathing techniques in hopes of better understanding some of the supernatural insights which were coming to light.[10] I found that mantra has direct ties to, and is derived from, Hinduism, so I began to study that religion also. I noticed that when I applied certain mantra techniques to my newfound abilities, I gained deeper levels of spiritual discernment, peace, tranquility, and understanding—not only within myself, but also within each of the supernatural abilities I'd been studying and practicing. I began to better see how I could experience the essence of the moment; I found that I could see myself, the experience, the moment,

9   Empirical: Philosophy derived as knowledge from experience, particularly from sensory observation, and not derived from the application of logic
10   Mantra: A sacred word, chant, or sound that is repeated during meditation to facilitate spiritual power and transformation of consciousness

and everything within it for exactly what it was. I recognize is it as I becoming *and* coming to know the knower.

Out-of-body experiences

Perhaps one of the most amazing experiences of all the types of psychic phenomena is OBEs (out-of-body experiences). Having the ability to separate from one's own body in a spiritual way is a truly instinctive and altogether natural aspect of who we are as humans. When we think of ourselves, we generally think of a mind, body, and spirit. As a whole, we are what we see in the mirror and what others see when they look upon us; however, when each part is scrutinized individually it eloquently reveals its truths. The truth is that the body cannot function without the mind, and our spirit that resides within connects to both; it allows for an unequivocal union between the three, for without any one of those we would cease to be who we are today. It's our consciousness that directs the mental and physical behavior of our bodies, and it could not do so without the essence of which we are—our soul and our spirit.

I studied and researched many instances where out-of-body experiences have been described, defined, and cataloged. I found out firsthand that although we are all capable of experiencing OBEs, not many of us are even willing to accept that they are a natural aspect of our lives. Through my empirical observations of OBEs, I have experienced earnest moments of reverence and a much greater understanding of spirituality.

Relative OBE

One of the first out-of-body experiences I can recall in great detail came about one evening while visiting a friend. We had come together for a social gathering on the weekend—

something we planned periodically. Typically it would be on a Saturday and we'd grill or barbeque outside and also cook over the stovetop, and as the evening progressed we would then congregate together in the living room and begin creating music. The evenings were extremely informal, but generally they would consist of a vocalist, electric guitar, acoustic guitar, and perhaps even a set of bongos. We would then all rotate between the instruments and take turns leading, singing, and creating in different genres of music. I believe the splendid melodies and lyrics leading into the moment may have even been the exact catalyst for my subsequent observation.

We were between sessions when I recall attaining a perfect state of bliss—a complete feeling of tranquility within the moment of observation. I sensed a connection and disconnection of the mind, body, and spirit that transpired simultaneously. It was at that exact moment that I not only stepped out-of-body, but stepped out so far that I could see the parameters of the actual moment of reality and existence from top to bottom. I paid close attention to each detail; I could see that reality had a distinct shape resembling a large rectangle with a fuzzy haze around the edges. All around the rectangular shape was a vast emptiness with a similar distinct haze and translucence. To the left I could visually see each moment that connected and led to the current specific moment (through both space and time). Each moment appeared as a rectangle within some great abyss. I realized I was looking at each moment in sequential succession, and I could see each moment flowing and attaching to each other, moment to moment. I then turned my head and gazed to the right and became aware of the future sequence of events in the same way. I was viewing the sum of all and every one of my actions in a successive order in both directions. I could see existence and space and time for the first time. Mesmerized with the understanding that there was a timeline of the past, present, and future, I then saw another figure by my side, but it was only visible from the incredible vantage point I had spiritually attained. I had miraculously gained a wonderful perspective and point of view of something and everything (that had been beyond my ability prior to that precise point in time). I felt I could see behind the veil of existence; and for the first time I had spiritually noticed that which appears to not visibly be there.

Another being

I could see a celestial being on the right side of my body, slightly above my shoulder but existing on another plane altogether. I noticed the presence directly affecting and witnessing every aspect of my actions and the decisions that I was making, and it was doing so without me directly knowing. It did not make its presence completely visible, I noticed it would periodically interact with me verbally in a form which sounded like a slight whisper.

One of the most impressive aspects of this supernatural being's voice, its whisper, is that it would accurately describe the last moment I had experienced at the same time that it would accurately describe the current moment I was experiencing, and would finally describe the moment that was to come. The whisper was encompassing my past, present, and future thoughts as they were directly being described in every intervening whisper in just one whisper. The understanding would come to light as the moment of the future became the past again, and the cycle would unfold and begin again and again, from moment to moment and time after time. I believe those whispers and brief interactions and this experience is but one small part of the ability that is sometimes referred to as clairvoyance.[11]

All of that transpired in but the twinkle of an eye. I still sat there on the couch with a musical instrument in my hands and my friends around me. That one moment had just yielded insight into the truth that there is another intricate part to each moment of our existences: Our emotions, thoughts, decisions, and actions lead to, and assist in, defining the reality of our existences. The fact that we all live separate lives, yet they all coincide and interconnect with one another, and all do so with an underlying divine company (such as the otherworldly spiritual presence), has led to some of my insights. Personally experiencing them showed me that God is with us in every moment and there is much more happening in each instance of life.

Three levels of OBE

It was soon after that observation when I noticed there were three different levels of an out-of-body state. I found that the OBE is a state of being that is attainable in many different ways, but it should be attained and entered into with the utmost care and focus—a focus which I believe can be established through concentration, meditation, devotion, belief, fasting, careful observation, and with an enlightened and metaphysical sensitivity.

The first of those levels is what I refer to as the "relative OBE perspective." I understand this to be when time and space are both evident, and the sum of one's actions and consequences are visible from moment to moment, in sequential order, in both directions.

The next level of OBE I call the "personal OBE perspective." It's where one has a perspective of oneself

11   Clairvoyance: The supposed ability to perceive things that are usually beyond the range of human senses

and one's surroundings, everything within, and everything that enters into one single moment.

Finally, the third level of OBE I refer to as a "transitional OBE perspective." It's where one is unattached to one's physical body yet can maneuver through any given space and time while remaining lucid. It combines both the relative and personal OBE perspectives.

Personal OBE

One of my first experiences of the personal OBE perspective transpired while I lay in bed and meditated on my physical surroundings. I had fasted for several days prior to that moment and prepared myself by utilizing breathing techniques, focused relaxation methods, and prayer. I then began to strive for the proper mindset of complete relaxation needed to attain a higher state of awareness, and the ability to connect and disconnect simultaneously. A higher state of spiritual awareness, extensive practice, meditation, and deeper levels of spiritual discernment must be achieved in order to obtain this type of out-of-body experience for extensive periods. [The proper attire is how I began to achieve the higher state of consciousness—clothes which are not made of synthetic fibers and stitching. I found synthetic clothing, or any uncomfortable clothing, may apply pressure to specific points on one's body that can disrupt one's natural flowing energy; it makes it more challenging to connect and disconnect to one's own body mentally, physically, and spiritually.]

When I stepped out-of-body, the first observation I noted was that although all the lights were off, everything within the room became slightly illuminated until it was entirely visible. I slowly began to rise until I was hovering nearly two feet above my physical body. As I stared in the direction of my feet, I saw something that I did not

19

understand right away: I saw a dark spirited being appear and begin floating towards me. The figure, which was within inches of my physical body, was translucent and rippled in a wave-like motion as it moved, but what was more startling to me was that it was completely black—it was a dark supernatural spirit. It began to hover directly over my physical body before moving from my feet towards my torso. I believed it was searching for an opportunity to do something very specific to me, perhaps harm. In the moment, I couldn't quite understand the significance of such a seemingly stealthy and perplexing force—one that clearly existed within our material world yet was from some other realm. It did not seem to be aware of me being in an out-of-body perspective; it seemed to be fixated on my physical body, and appeared to be searching for the right moment to attack by observing and searching for weak links in my mental and spiritual armor. [What I had previously experienced of those types of beings was that they would become aggressive towards those with negative emotions and scattered thoughts, which can make for a very uncomfortable experience. I thought it to be what has been referred to as an incubus; incubi seem to be attracted to, and feed off of, fear.[12] I found that the best form of self-defense came in the form of faith, prayer, and light. I also learned that by staying faithful in a positive emotional state and being fearless, one will always persevere over such encounters.]

The out-of-body moment lasted only for a brief period of time, but within the experience I realized that everything is illuminated and is always completely visible. Whether it's during daytime's sunlight or in complete darkness, everything can be and is always seen. With the proper mindset, faith, and eagerness, one can attain such

---

12   Incubus: Something that causes somebody much worry or anxiety, especially a nightmare or obsession

a vantage point of visibility with that particular out-of-body perspective.

As I descended back into my body from my slightly higher vantage point, I noticed my breathing was extremely shallow and I felt myself to be in complete peace, perhaps from the breathing practices I had been utilizing. Upon arriving back to my body I noticed the room was dark again, and having transitioned, I made the observation that when we experience a particular out-of-body perspective (as we ascend in any motion, either directional or temporal), we do so from our mind with emotional recognition of one focal point.

The transitional OBE

The transitional OBE perspective transpired initially in the same way as the personal out-of-body perspective. I prepared myself through relaxation techniques and a positive frame of mind until I reached a perfect state of bliss—those relaxation methods contribute directly to establishing such connections and disconnections simultaneously. While in that higher state of awareness, and when one obtains and reaches his highest order and pinnacle; this type of OBE allows for an extraordinary capability to flourish—one gains the ability to spiritually maneuver through one's physical surroundings, both directional and temporal.

The first time that type of OBE experience entranced me, I was alone in my bedroom and had been focusing my studies on psychic and supernatural awareness. I was practicing an exercise which allowed for focus, clarity of the moment, and vision within oneself and of every moment—a type of psychic forecasting.[13] I was lying on my bed, as I often do when meditating and listening to

13   Psychic forecasting: Predicting the future using psychic techniques

music, and as I reached a pinnacle moment, I felt a distinct disconnection from my physical body and I could visibly see my hands appear to be moving away from me. I had fixated on them, knowing that the out-of-body experience would soon reveal itself. I could feel that my spirit was moving away from my physical body. I was hovering above where I lay and I could visibly see myself below. The movement I had attained was free-flowing, meaning I could move about the room without any difficulty. I could rise to a higher point within the room simply by thinking of it, and when I felt or thought of being in another part of the room, I felt myself begin to float there. I was completely aware of my surroundings and my place within the moment. As I looked in the direction of the window, which had the curtains drawn and closed, I could see directly outside. It appeared as if there was no window there at all, nor any curtains drawn and blocking the view. The fact that it was nighttime and that there was no light present made no difference. I could see everything in great detail—the large tree twenty feet outside of my window, the fence twenty feet behind the tree, the green grass on the ground, and the color of the leaves that lay on the ground. Everything was slightly illuminated. I had attained incredible sight and vision. I could see everything everywhere within the moment.

I moved towards the direction of the window, or at least where I understood the window appeared to be. Not only was there no visible sign of the window, but there appeared to be no wall there either. I was floating about four feet above the ground and when I decided to move in the direction of the yard next door, I felt myself instantaneously moving in that direction. As the fence approached, I seemed to pass right through it and into the next yard. I looked around and felt complete. I could sense every movement of everything within the moment.

At that point I noticed I was beginning to move faster than I had moved while indoors. I also had the ability to see in different directions as I traveled, and was able to navigate in that new way simply while thinking of a direction, and could travel in it for as long as I thought to. Everything was again illuminated and visible while in this out-of-body state. Not once did I have a thought of not being able to return to my body, nor did I fear being unable to maneuver anywhere I thought. I decided to further observe the out-of-body perspective around the house, so I went in search of any constraints and, surprisingly, I found none. I also found that when I simply thought of being inside my room and opening my eyes, I was instantly back within my body and realizing my return.

The proper mindset is absolutely crucial to discovering such spiritual knowledge and insights. My glimpses were an intricate part of the opportunity to awaken spiritually into life again. The spiritual journey of awareness was brought forth from God, the Father of all creation, and was achieved partially through meditations, but ultimately with focus and God's permission.

I would strongly compare that feeling—of the awakening of oneself, and the experience of being on a path lined with many supernatural and celestial moments of discovery— to being born again. Perhaps that and other spiritual awakenings are indeed an invitation, an opportunity to learn and discover our true selves and our true purposes in life. Those of us who have been fortunate enough thus far to have experienced such an occurrence (of feeling an impelling force and sudden urges to connect with something greater than ourselves) can perhaps identify with many aspects of those findings. For those of us who have yet to (or who have not allowed ourselves to) experience such occurrences, perhaps learning of those aspects in greater detail will allow for a better understanding of those of us who do. They may, in fact, help us all to recognize each of those moments as it arrives.

These amazing occurrences transpire within us all every day, all the time. They are here to assist us in the world. It was through my inquiries and lessons that I found the narrowest path—the path which has been difficult yet amazing, filled with every emotion I've ever experienced. When tied altogether and interpreted, that knowledge and those experiences have made me who I am; without any of them I would not be who I am today. *All thanks to God.*

The Magic of Prescience

I had always been interested in the science of matter and energy and in the relationship between them. I can recall being an astute student of human behavior and of the interactions we commonly share with all objects. It was with that interest that I began studying prescience, clairvoyance, and magic—true magic. I began by researching the origins of the word magic. I researched many magicians and found that most were simply entertainers and performers using legerdemain to pass off misdirection and staged illusions for truly supernatural skills and techniques.[14] I then found that the word magic originally referred to an early mountain people called the Magi or Zoroastrians. They are said to have had the ability of true magic and could predict the future; they knew about important and insightful things. Some of the Zoroastrians or Magi are referenced within the Bible as the three wise men who traveled to visit Jesus after his birth and gave him gifts

---

14   Legerdemain: Sleight of hand or a display of skill or adroitness

of gold, frankincense, and myrrh. There are many early accounts of Magi that gained much notability in the mid-fifth century—they are said to be a part of the six tribes the population of Media was divided into. The Magi are an ancient people who I believe tapped into a divine ability (we all possess) in order to gain spiritual insights and knowledge and better direct their community. It is also said that the Zoroastrians or Magi were known to be the first true missionaries. I incorporated these ancient and divine spiritual practices/methods into my research.

The experiments

Having read and studied numerous subjects ranging from quantum to particle physics, I decided to conduct several experiments and tests.[15,16] I believed that verifiable and reproducible results could possibly help lead to, and identify, noticeable and key attributes in the study of mystical and supernatural phenomena. I hoped that with physics I could help uncover a missing, and elusive attribute in my understanding of prescience.[17]

I began by noting what I would need in order to create a type of laboratory and what I would need to perform, identify, verify, and reproduce measurable results within the study of prescience and ESP. Using the means available to me, my bedroom became a type of laboratory for each exercise, but with different elements for each measurement. Perhaps one evening would require the lights on, while another evening would require the lights off. One exercise might require furniture relocations and room alterations, while another would require clothing changes and object rearrangements within any given moment. Other exercises

15   Quantum: The smallest unit used to measure a physical property. For example, the quantum of electromagnetic radiation is the photon.
16   Particle: Any one of the basic units of matter, e.g. a molecule, atom, or electron
17   Prescience: Knowledge of actions or events before they happen

28

would not require any changes at all. I had begun to purposefully alter aspects of each moment in hopes of identifying the key attributes and constants to each one. I would carefully observe each moment's changes while I also searched for the constants within each moment. I began researching and performing the tests with a very important verse that I believe to be an extremely important foundation of life:

> *"Ask, and it will be given to you; seek,*
> *and you will find; knock, and it will be*
> *opened to you"* (MATTHEW 7:7).

I often began each exercise with that verse, followed by much meditation and spiritual preparation for entering into a higher state of consciousness. The meditation process would generally begin with the focus on each hoped-for result; it was a complete mental assimilation of visualization and expectancy.

I maintained a mental perspective and record of the results obtained, and what I found was that not only were the results becoming more predictable, but they were becoming more predictable because of an incredible force which began to show me mental visualizations and audible revelations of each truthful moment a mere fraction of a second before each actual moment transpired. I had somehow begun to see and hear each moment prior to actually reaching it.

Playing cards

The initial tool I decided upon for each of those exercises was a simple deck of playing cards. Each deck of playing cards, as you know, comes with fifty-two cards and two jokers—a standard deck. I would begin by removing both jokers, and then I would shuffle the deck profusely. I would then set the goal of discovering the ace from each suit, and then I would attempt to choose each subsequent card without replacing each prior card I had removed.

The probability equation for randomly pulling a specified card from within a deck of cards and specifically acquiring the card you want is:

$$Pr(a)=4/52=1/13, Pr(b)(a)=3/51=1/17, Pr(c)(b)(a)=2/50=1/25, Pr(d)(c)(b)(a)=1/49=1/49 \text{ "}1/13 \times 1/17 \times 1/25 \times 1/49=270,725\text{"}$$

What is important to consider and keep in mind is that as the number of cards decreases, due to the previous cards being discovered and removed, the odds increase exponentially of not being capable of actual discovery—another important aspect for anyone who may believe in coincidence.

There are several factors which must be adhered to in order to achieve those types of intrepid perceptions. One must possess proper consciousness, and (what I have found is that) each moment must contain a multitude of positive emotions, ranging from exuberance to felicity, all encompassed by faith and penitence. I believe having such a mindset is a must in obtaining such astonishing results, in those tests or anything else in life.

From the outset, I noticed that I had an instinctive ability to discover each card I focused upon. I could lay the entire deck of cards in a straight line, reach into the deck of cards, and pull out the correct card I thought about. Those types of results were not always instant, but after several decks of cards and several months of practice, I was astonished at how palpable the results seemed to have become. I could focus on any card(s) and produce the same type of result again and again. I realized I had tapped into the real nature of the highest order of truth. I found that while in that meditative state of higher awareness, and while focusing on the expected result, I could shuffle and then split the deck into several groups—two groups on the left and two groups on the right—and still I was able to reach into the correct group and find each specific card I was thinking about. It was around that time that I began to delve more deeply into prescience and understand how we perceive and interact with such a divine force.

Prescience

Prescience is defined as the human knowledge of actions or events before they happen. I understood the experience as knowing without knowing. Many of us often experience that type of phenomenon through intuition, instinct, or extrasensory perception and simply dismiss it as coincidence. I decided to test, observe, and note that ability. I had always subscribed to the theory of cause and effect: for every action there is an equal and opposite reaction. I believed that all I needed to do was open myself up to the possibilities of prescience and recognize and record the differences within each finding. Through that I hoped to find the key attribute that seemed to be so elusive.

Still working with the cards, I would periodically change the lessons by adding candlelight and altering the way in which I discovered each card. I found that I could shuffle the entire deck of cards, scatter them face down, and still immediately locate each specific card I searched for. I could literally feel the cards internally, within my head and my being, and I began to act as one within each moment; I truly felt that each playing card was a direct extension of my being. I could mentally visualize each card I was hoping to locate within the deck before moving towards its actual location. I had entered into a mental and spiritual state of bliss; and it was there, in that utopian stillness, that I noticed a distinct intrinsic attribute of karmic predictability.[18]

A translucent light

I was searching for an explanation to better describe how and why such moments of prescience exist and flourish, when I noticed what appeared to be small bright and translucent spheres. The extremely tiny, white spheres appeared suddenly and for a very brief period of time. In each instance, it would often surround the edges of the correct card I was thinking of. I believed it was a very specific way in which God was showing me the path. The duration of the spheres' presence would conclude within fractions of a second, but it was in those moments that prescience took on a whole new meaning. That feeling or hunch of intuition was beginning to give way to an inherent visual perception.[19]

The sphere was incredibly small, and was translucent in appearance. It glistened, as if indicating a strong sense of vitality. By that point I could see that its presence was visible within every other scenario of life. The small, translucent

18   Karma: In Hindu and Buddhist philosophy, the quality of some-body's current and future lives as determined by that person's behavior in the and in previous lives
19   Inherent: Existing in someone or something as a permanent and inseparable element, quality, or attribute

light-colored sphere was around almost everything I was inquisitive of and inclined to discover—it seemed to lay out a subliminal path that was visible and comprehendible if I intently focused diligently enough, and then added the proper mindset or state of mind—which is positive exuberance and felicitous expectancy, all encompassed with faith.

These tiny lights of energy that appeared from beyond the yonder intrigued me, and I took it upon myself to further test them. Almost right away, I was able to deduce that when I was truly focused on finding any specific card (and while maintaining proper consciousness) I could even find it in the dark. I could turn my head in a different direction, or close my eyes, and it made no difference; I could simply find it. I felt the essence of my being and my subconscious were instinctively drawn to (the real nature and essence of the highest order of truth), these spheres, and my being instinctively knew how to reach them, and I knew right then that everything was and is possible. While we all possess the abilities within us to participate in such miraculous moments of prescience, often we do so without recognition of its occurrence–they are an interaction between the essence of our being and the highest order of truth, that allow us to find and follow the path in our heart, all thanks to God.

Tarot

I decided that since I had been able to associate such dazing perceptions with fate and karmic predictability, the next best and logical tool for observation would likely be a deck of tarot cards. I had been given a deck several years earlier, and I chose to extend my research with them because of their ability to predict fatum and their karmic associations to prescience.[20] I decided to move forward without knowing the origins, or even having a great understanding of, the tarot or how to interpret what each card represented. I figured I could learn to interpret them with my emotions and with the insights which had been assisting me in each of my previous experiences.

I decided to utilize the same techniques as I had before, beginning by aligning myself with proper consciousness and then focusing on a specific thought with an underlying question: Who am I, and how is this possible? I meditated for several minutes on that question and then shuffled the cards profusely. I reached into the tarot card deck and pulled out a single card, turned it over and read "The Star." I immediately searched online for the definition of "The Star" card. To my amazement the definition read: You have beheld the soul of nature and nothing will ever be impossible for you.

By that point I had a better sense of the path I'd found, but as we all know, there is a difference between knowing the path and walking the path; there is action required in order to fully understand such insightful knowledge.

Matter and energy is balanced throughout the universe, and life is filled with examples of that balance—from yin and yang to the positive and the negative.[21] In order to gain insight into how we perceive and interact with this perfect balance, we must be fearless of it. I bring that to attention because despite my beautiful experiences, I realized that without the proper mindset, I ran the

20   Fatum (Latin); n. Destiny, fate, (of a god) speech
21   Yin and yang: Yin is the principle of darkness, negativity, and femininity in Chinese philosophy that is the counterpart of yang. Yang is the principle of light, heat, motivation, and masculinity. The dual, opposite, and complementary principles of yin and yang are thought to exist in varying proportions in all things.

risk of changing a happy moment into a fearful one. Without fully understanding this balance, one can become susceptible to specious emotions/lies.[22] Specious emotions are distinctively recognizable—they are raucously intertwined with one's emotional perspective, and they can cause confusion and uncertainty, which can lead to doubt and fear. Negative thoughts and emotions can bring one's worst fears to fruition, and leave one in a tremulous state of being for as long as one is willing to subscribe to such a diverging mindset; anything other than the proper mindset of (positive exuberance and felicitous expectancy, all encompassed with faith) could disrupt the balance and lead to that tremulous state of uncertainty. In layman's terms, the continuance of positive emotions can bring us closer to the divine within, whereas specious emotions can lead us into a tremulous state of uncertainty to be without.

Collective consciousness

A place of collective consciousness exists for us all; a place where absolute truth resides and where we all connect and interact spiritually. For now I'll call it a vestibule with many doorways. We're all capable of visiting it and meeting others there, and many of us already do so, knowingly or unknowingly, despite not understanding anything about its existence. Many insights have come to light for me there, they have come in the form of visions, prophecy, and miracles. This place has often felt like being in a dream, only I'm awake. Most of my visits have been seen in a clairvoyant manner and at other times in a spiritual and psychic way, which I shall describe later. This place of collective consciousness exists alongside and within the material world in which we all live in, and its entrance

---

22   Specious: Appearing to be true but really false

points are here, there, and everywhere. We all are granted access, but in order for us to enter, we must open our eyes and have faith, believe that it truly exists, and then acknowledge it.

Visions

Ever since my initial findings, I have undergone many intriguing and humbling moments. One of the earliest signs of spirituality I experienced, along that journey of discovery and while searching for understanding, came to me in the form of visions. Each vision specifically pertained to experiences that were either a part of my life or aspects of others' lives, which I would directly affect or be affected by. I noticed that the visions would often happen in a place unlike any place I'd seen before—a place where room after room and doorway after doorway would reveal incredible insights into the unknown. Some of the earliest visions I experienced while in that higher state of prophetic awareness were extremely difficult to understand. They were visual images that I viewed as a quick flash, but the flash would be intertwined with several other yet-to-be-experienced, segments of my life. I found that the common factor which each of the visions shared was that they would come to fruition, generally speaking, within the subsequent twelve hours.

I studied those visions for several months intensely searching for specific patterns which I believed could help lead to predictability and a better understanding of how to experience such a phenomenon. I found that even after the first several months of study, the only time I was able to recognize what I was seeing within the visions was at their moments of actualization. I had hoped there was some sign or event that could possibly precede the actualization of each vision, which encouraged me to become a student of déjà vu and intuition.

I began to also study fate, karma, and the force that predetermines events more intently. I found that no matter which particular monotheistic religion or spirituality one follows, understanding that a place of collective consciousness exists is the most crucial part of recognizing such visions. In that place of truth and understanding, the place where it happens before it happens, we connect with and talk with one another before important moments happen in our lives. The place exists to better assist us all in choosing the direction our lives shall proceed in.

When we enter into the spiritual place of collective consciousness, mostly unbeknownst to us, we connect and interact with others on a deeply spiritual level. We talk through and arrive at our fate spiritually before we act it out in the material world. I found that sharing the truth about our own lives does not automatically give us precedence over all other subjects or events within that place. We share all of God's creation with everyone else, and because our lives and their individual timelines interconnect, it's crucial that we be respectful and kind to those we meet there. We must fully grasp and understand that the sum of our own actions doesn't always take precedence over everything else in these spiritual meetings or in physical life.

A spiritual premonition

When the visions first began, I noticed they came in a few different ways. As I described earlier, they could flash briefly or could appear as if I was dreaming but still awake (in the form of a premonition).

I can recall having such a spiritual premonition and vision of my grandfather, Lefty. He was an athlete who played baseball most of his life: he was known as a left-handed home run hitter; and that's where he got the nickname of Lefty. He worked on his farm just outside of Dallas, Texas, until his mid-seventies, when he then moved back to Austin and lived out an incredible life near most of his family.

By the time of the story, he was ninety-six. I would stop by his house weekly and visit. We would often share stories and each other's company, laughing and talking about our pasts and our futures. When it was time for me to leave, he would wish me well and tell be to be careful; then I would shake his hand, give him a kiss on the forehead, tell him I loved him, and say goodbye. Approximately two months before he passed, I had a premonition of my grandfather. I had been thinking of him often in the months before his passing and I could sense something different; I thought that perhaps his time here on earth was nearly at hand. I spoke with my parents in regards to those thoughts and told them I had recently had a vision of Lefty lying on his back in another room. I walked to his side and grabbed a hold of his hand and witnessed his death. I somehow knew that his time would come soon and that I would be there when it did.

When I received that premonition, I began to visit with him more often than once a week—I wanted to spend more time with him, knowing that he could go at any moment. Lefty began asking me, jokingly, if I was lost or something. He had a great sense of humor. When his time was near, he asked everyone over for a weekend gathering. It was the Sunday before he passed, and our family gathered to celebrate his life. Most of his children were there and almost all his grandchildren; even some of his great-grandchildren were near him on that last weekend. It was while we were visiting with him that Sunday when he mentioned that he had just dry-cleaned his favorite suit. He mentioned to us all that it was in his closet and then expressed that he wanted to be buried in it. Jokingly he told us to not put shoes on him when it was his time to be buried because he thought they could benefit someone who really needed them. We all stayed until sunset, laughing and sharing great moments of our lives with him. It was one of the last times we all gathered together as a family.

Within forty-eight hours of that final meeting with his family, Lefty began to transition; his body was reaching its end. Hospice was called to assist as he slipped into a sleeping state of consciousness. He awoke several times as family members arrived to be at his side. The final time his eyes opened was when I was standing by his side. I held his hand tightly, and as he squeezed mine his eyes opened. We stared at each other for several minutes. I began thinking telepathically to him, mentally telling him that I loved him very much. Then I thought to him once again, telling him it was going to be alright, that there was nothing to be afraid of, and that he should not fear what was next. Then I said to him aloud,

"I love you," and surprisingly he answered back.

He said, "I love you."

Those were his very last words. Within minutes his eyes would close and not open again.

That Thursday morning at around 3:30 a.m., his house was filled with his family; but my aunt, his daughter, and I were the only ones awake. As my aunt and I stayed up talking and telling stories to keep each other awake, something began to happen in the corner of the room. I could see out of the corner of my eye that Lefty's arms had begun to rise up. I immediately pointed that out to my aunt and we both rushed to his side and held his hands. He began to bend his arms at the elbow and then raised them up as we held his hands. He gripped our hands with all his strength for around twenty seconds, and then he took his final breath and slowly began to lay his arms down until he had passed on. My aunt and I both began to cry, but it was just as it was meant to be and it was just as I had envisioned it several months before. I'd had that exact premonition and I thought it to be a truly reverential blessing to be a part of his life and of his death. I was honored to have shared all the time I had with him. He was and will always be one of my heroes.

I share the prophetic blessing with you, and I hope and pray that you may all open your eyes, hearts, and minds to the endless possibilities of every moment; and that you give thanks and praise to the Lord our God and understand that tomorrow is promised to no one.

A sacred place

The place of collective consciousness is specifically carved out in this life for premonitions and visions and the like. It's where our consciousness connects to the past, present, and future of our reality. It exists within our world and it is a place with many doors and passageways leading into and off of it. Holy men and women, shamans, spiritualists, the divine, the pious, navigators, and prophets alike consider the place sacred.

For many of us, having such insightful understandings can be somewhat overwhelming at first, but I've found that the more boldly one embraces such truthful moments, the more one is able to obtain a connection to future events. They may come as a result of fate, karma, mystical interactions, or spiritual unions, and they may come with a wondrous glimmer of who (and why) we are from one day to the next; but understand they do so. *All thanks to God.*

Miracles

The higher state of prophetic awareness I have been describing and sharing is not only revealed in the form of visions, but also in our ability to ascertain and comprehend anything supremely well, such as miracles. I believe that everything is a miracle, from the very inclination of creation to infinity. The fact that we can explain away many truths does not make them less than such.

Within a year of my grandfather Lefty passing on, another family member who had battled an illness for several months suddenly became deathly ill. She was admitted to the hospital with her health rapidly deteriorating. While in the hospital, she also developed an infection of her blood (MRSA) and was battling excruciating pain caused by the shingles on her skin.[23] I had gone to the hospital to visit with her and to check on her well-being, hoping for her recovery to be soon, but she was not able to get out of bed at all. I stayed only for a short period of time, wished her well, and then left, and then reality began to set in . . . I realized that there was a distinct possibility she may not recover at all. Later that evening I began to pray for her and asked God if I could help her in any way, or if I could alleviate any pain she may be suffering from. I specifically asked God if I could carry any burden or pain she may have. I hadn't ever asked anything like it from God before, but it felt like the right thing to ask for.

When I awoke, I noticed I had a strange feeling on my back. At first the pain was near my right shoulder blade. It felt like a sore muscle or a deep bruise, so I took a couple of aspirin and went about my normal day. It was later that evening when I felt the pain move from my right shoulder to my abdomen, at which point the pain had

---

23   MRSA: A strain of a common infection-causing bacterium that has become resistant to treatment by the antibiotic methicillin and is therefore a hazard in places such as hospitals

become excruciating and nauseatingly intense. Patches of skin began to change and discolor as they bubbled up in a line stretching from my lower abdomen to my lower right shoulder blade. I had never felt such pain before in my entire life. I realized then that I had contracted shingles, and when I thought back to what I had asked from God, I felt truly blessed. The moment was a truly humbling experience, and one of the first times I felt that I could physically see God working in my life. There may be a logical explanation as to how I contracted shingles—my aunt was at my house days before all that happened, and she may have used a towel that I used after washing it. The fact remains, however, that I had hoped to help my aunt and had prayed to alleviate her pain in any way, so for me to awaken with that sensation the morning after I had prayed to help my aunt was a true miracle to experience.

I lay in bed for quite some time that morning, meditating and practicing many spiritual awareness techniques—and as I lay there and prayed and gave thanks to God for answering a prayer that I believed truly helped my aunt, I had a vision of my aunt entering my room, which was followed by what I believe to be a holy moment. I could see she was in an astral form and in a wheelchair, but what surprised me was that as she rolled closer to me I could hear her talking to me. We observed each other for a several moments, as if to simply acknowledge each other, or think hello, and within a few minutes she was gone. I believe that my spiritual awareness and an understanding of this grand vestibule and collective consciousness helped to allow the vision to become recognizable. As I lay there hoping to make sense of the meeting, I realized it would perhaps be one of the last times I saw her alive. I was astonished yet filled with excitement at the encounter, but God must have wanted to bless me even more, because at that moment I felt a presence in the room with me. It was at that moment that I truly became aware; it was when I heard a distinct voice say,

"You are in God's grace."

The voice was loud and clear and it seemed to come from another standing right next to me. I didn't know what to do, nor how to respond. I felt many emotions and many thoughts had come to mind all at once, and then a mental conversation began. I was eager to ask who the celestial being was and why it was possible for me to see it, but then I realized I already had a strong feeling of knowing those answers, so our conversation graciously moved to one of earnest spirituality with questions regarding my past studies and experiences.

I learned of many insights that evening and realized I had become part of a miracle, and a true supernatural perception of life that included the past, present, and future. I also realized at that point that those spiritual meetings were leading to something quite special. I was asked if I had any questions for God. I was told that because of where I was within life, I could not yet see him or understand him directly, and that if I had any questions they would be passed through the supernatural being that I had begun to converse with. I was told that I could ask anything. My response was,

"No. I don't have any questions at the moment. Whatever God may have planned for me is exactly the way it will be."

The spiritual meeting lasted for several hours with many insights into the supernatural, and it concluded when I got tired and said goodnight.

My aunt survived for several more days after being a part of that miracle. Although I could not speak to her while the blessing of taking her sickness was transpiring,

I believe with all that I am that I helped alleviate some of her pain in that special way. I had never before been a part of something so wondrous—it truly changed my life and my understanding of the grace of God. I set about to learn as much as I could about the other world within our world. The more often I entered such a spiritual labyrinth, the more of its details became clearer to me. I began to notice that while in a higher state of prophetic awareness and while maintaining the proper consciousness, I could spiritually meet with enigmatic individuals who seemed to form spiritually right before my eyes. Fine particles of shimmering vitality shaped themselves into the celestial embodiment of translucent light-covered figures which would then glisten and careen effortlessly and gracefully at the speed of emotion and thought. They would move about, approach curiously and then pass alongside me; then they would revert back into a fine mist of particles and vanish, all in an instant.

At that point I wasn't quite sure what the significance of the interactions was, what they would lead to, or even what I hoped they would reveal. I simply knew that my perceptions of these encounters were beyond the natural range of most human senses, and that the celestial embodiments were of a significantly high importance in regards to understanding the interconnectivity we all seem to directly share. I had always believed anything is possible, and then became even more mesmerized each time I pointed that ability at several other frequently observed phenomena.

Photographs

The next observation was of a different kind of phenomenon—something I had not seen before that was now becoming recognizable when I looked at all photographs. As I gazed upon the many pictures I had placed before me for observation I could see that I was in some of the photos and I that had also been the one to take some of them. The images in my personal photos seemed to come alive as I gazed upon them. They began to show the past, present, and future moments that directly surrounded the exact moment when the photo was taken. I was completely enthralled. I noticed those same types of results were also recognizable within every other image and photo I viewed. Not only that, I recognized the visible presence of something moving at such great speeds (as with around almost everything else everywhere within life) and within all the photos. I was puzzled as to how and why. I made some mental notes and continued searching for a better explanation as to what it was and how it was all possible, and then I moved forward.

Water

I understood that having been born under the water sign of Pisces, I had always been attracted to the supernatural (as I expect most people are). I practiced and experienced all the usual tendencies that are associated with a person born on March 1st, but I noticed another way to perceive and interpret wondrous events of the past, present, and future through water. I found that (just like seers of the past who could look into crystal balls, or onto a body of water, and focus intently on events yet unknown), I could enter a higher state of prophetic awareness, focus on the translucence of the water, and it would begin to give way to visions and images. The images would appear in brief flashes, like a movie or a short film. Sometimes they would show pending events, or even show events that were happening in real time; or they would show events that had already transpired in the past.

One of the most puzzling aspects of having visions in the form of a flash, premonition, translucent image or a waking dream was trying to decipher between them all and to understand exactly what was being shown. Only the seer has the ability to properly interpret what he/she sees, and to determine when and how each revelation should be understood and acted upon if, in fact, there is a need to do so.

Rest assured that all visions are real and have been an important aspect of our lives from the very beginning. They should be held in high regard. I also believe that if there is a recognizable task which has been given, we have the responsibility to act upon it in a positive manner or suffer the consequences of not following the chosen path for our lives. By acting on our visions, we will grow and continuously move in a more positive direction, as we learn who we are in this amazing world and also while we come to understand just how very blessed we are to be alive.

Energy and Chakras

When I first began observing what a wonderful world we live in, I noticed another underlying force common to everything and every moment. We all produce and exert energy, and I began to notice it in every form. I noticed its tranquil, sometimes harmonious properties, and at other times its transformation of form, which can cause vigorous action in both positive and negative ways. Having a relative understanding of matter and energy and our relationship between them, I understood that energy cannot be destroyed; it simply changes form, characteristics, or properties. It was with those principles in mind that I observed many subjects in their relation to energy. I noted their outcomes and effects, not only on myself, but on everything incorporating any given moment.

There is much we don't know about certain forms of energy, or how some of those forms even really work. We know that it is possible for something as small as a subatomic particle to generate copious amounts of energy through a chain reaction when split, or that certain forms of energy (such as light) can travel through space as both particles and waves; but as we observe the human body, there are surprisingly many unanswered questions regarding energy.[24] Energy is in our lives at every moment—in every waking moment, and even while we sleep at night, there are forces at work around and within us. As I empirically researched the human body from a metaphysical and spiritual viewpoint, I began scrutinizing each insight with the hopes of gaining more understanding of human energy. These burgeoning empathic methods were deeply rooted in spirituality and in enlightenment.

A dream

As my search for a better understanding continued, I had a dream. I was standing at the base of a softly sloping hill. I first noticed the landscape, which was full of tall overgrown grass, and then the green tree canopy hanging ever so close to the ground. I turned my head to the left and, to my surprise, saw another figure standing there before me. I recognized it to not be human; I knew from all the visits I had been having that perhaps it could be otherworldly, and it was standing on a path lined with stairs. The stairs were carved into the slope of the hill. This being noticed me observing them and quickly ran up the stairs, and just as it reached the top of the hill, it turned around and threw a bright spherical light at me that glistened and sparkled as it came closer and closer swirling as it traveled faster and faster. Just as it reached me, I opened my eyes from my dream and instantly realized that the light was actually

24   Particles and waves: According to Einstein, light is composed of photons—small packets of energy. Light exhibits both a wave theory and a particle theory at the same time. For the most part, light behaves like a wave. Light waves are also called electromagnetic waves because they are made up of both electric (E) and magnetic (H) fields.

a particle that had been emitted from the conversion of hydrogen to helium which took place on the sun. The fact that it had traveled ninety-three million miles across space as both a packet and wave of light, and then found its way through my blinds and landed on my eyes and entered into my dream, causing me to wake up, astonished me. I was amazed, first with the idea that the nuclear furnace called our sun had converted eight hundred million tons of hydrogen into helium in a single second, and secondly that that had started a chain reaction that would combine with my dream to wake me up precisely at the moment the light particle from the sun and the light from the dream both seemed to arrive simultaneously.

Waves of light

My fascination with energy and the different forms it takes when traveling had arisen from being able to sense energy as it is generated, dissipated, conjugated, and radiated. I began this portion of my studies with one of the biggest and most obvious points of energy in all our lives: the sun. Although it is extremely far from earth, its energy is utilized in many ways by just about everything that exists on our planet. It's difficult to imagine life without it; however, its energy generates and radiates and travels ninety-three million miles simply to reach earth. It's hard to fathom the distance its energy travels every second, let alone the fusion process which must take place for it to do so.

On observation, I clearly noticed light particles traveling in packets of four, and I noted the characteristics of the light's refractions off of things such as water and liquid, lightly-colored objects, and even solid objects. This helped lead me to notice energy waves emitted from not only light, sound, heat, and magnets, but ultimately from everything that has an energy signature.

Waves of sound

While in that season of discovery, I would lie in bed daily and begin to meditate, pray, and prepare myself for the day's observations. As the nighttime approached, I began practicing mantra breathing techniques, focusing on the energy waves and patterns that I anticipated seeing with the next encounter. I really wasn't too sure what to expect or what I would notice, when I suddenly would began mentally picturing waves of energy moving before my eyes. I could sense that the energy waves were similar in form to ocean waves. I could feel their energy, and as I focused on their shape and motion, I closed my eyes. As I lay there, noticing between each breath the sound wave, I could hear a familiar buzzing sound resonating from the closet—the buzz was coming from a box in the closet that housed the old doorbell mechanism. The doorbell had broken many years earlier, and the buzzing sound had been resonating from the box ever since.

Energy waves

For the first time, I was able to differentiate between each energy wave within a moment. I first noticed the energy wave coming from the doorbell mechanism, which was consistent with the path of alternating current, and it traveled in a steady and continuous form. I was then able to align and synchronize my heartbeat and my breath with the motion of its energy wave and move with what felt like to be in unison with it. While doing so, I visibly observed the energy wave, and I could trace its path as it moved throughout the room and bounced off objects. Each wave travelled like a ripple of water, but it did so unapparent to the naked eye.

Again I lay there sensing everything. I noticed other types of energy patterns present in the room, but one stood out more than the others. Although I could sense the vibrations and motions of the light which came from the LED on the radio, and visibly see its motion as it moved in waves and in packets and refracted off each wall; and I could feel and see the motion of sound that came from the buzzing in the closet and which moved around the room bouncing off each object and each wall; I found the most interesting energy was coming from within.

Energy signatures

I began to observe my central nervous system and its actions and reactions and interactions, both in and outside of my body, as I applied different emotions and thoughts. I imagined myself into different scenarios and with different thoughts—both positive and negative. Again, I thought of energy and how it simply changes form, and of how the neurological system of the brain and the central nervous system both operate off of electrical pulses.

I began looking for the specific energy signature that the body produces when an action or reaction occurs due to particular thoughts, and then what would transpire when emotional and physical scenarios and interactions were in play.

I found that when I pinch the palm of my hand, the energy exerted by my index finger and thumb causes the nerve within my hand to transmit an electrical pulse through my arm, into my spine, and up to my brain via the central nervous system.[25] The pulse is then converted

25   Central nervous system: The part of the nervous system, con-
sisting of the brain and spinal cord, that controls and coordinates most
functions of the body and mind. Impulses from sense organs travel to the
central nervous system and impulses to muscles and glands travel from it.

to knowledge through interpretation, which at that point changes form—from a pulse into a thought rooted in emotion (in this case it was discomfort) which then spreads and transmits out from the brain as both an energy wave and a sound. Our thoughts are generated by a number of different stimulants, and they allow us to not only reason by comparison, but to hold and transmit an electrical signature that is not only visible but also interpretable, if carefully observed and scrutinized. Our thought patterns give way to faint and distinctive underlying sound and the entire process works through energy. Having just learned to visibly see the motion of energy, I was able to interpret simultaneously what I was seeing and hearing in others on a whole new level.

Energy does not cease to exist; once exerted it simply changes its form. The action or reaction from the pinch on my palm generated an electrical occurrence and pulse that traveled along its conducted path, the central nervous system, to the brain. Upon first noticing that all thoughts send out its own sound and energy, I realized that each letter of the alphabet produces a signature sound, and with that understanding I found that I could interpret each letter's energy signature—the sound and decibel level of each letters and words all would carry a distinct energy wave, signature, and sound. It was also at that point that I began to teach myself how to interpret and distinguish between the different energy signatures I could see and hear.

Emotional imprints

As we travel through space and time here on earth, our bodies leave a type of energy wave imprint similar to the wave a boat leaves as it travels across a body of water. Many people have the ability to sense unique vibrations, and to interpret the energy of any given moment and place, which I believe is partly due to the emotional attachments we have to every moment. I have been able to deduce that our emotions and our thoughts are an extremely important part of each moment, and that they are crucial to our future paths in life. Our emotions and thoughts not only assist in guiding us on our journey in life; they help determine our paths by utilizing our positive or negative feeling, thus guiding and revealing our course. I consider our emotions as powerful as our thoughts and words, all of which hold, release, and exert a distinct energy. The energy leaves emotional traces behind or, in some cases, even produces a strong-enough energy signature that's detectable many miles away, just like an echo.

Spiritual energy imprints

One intriguing energy imprint I noticed happened late one evening while the moon was full. I had been living very near a lake in the country, and at the back of the property was a natural freshwater spring which fed into a small pond which fed into the lake. The beauty of the place was remarkable, and it was easy to see why anyone would call it home. It provided shelter from the elements, had its own natural water supply, and had an abundant food source of wild deer that often drank from the springs. The spring was located nearly a hundred yards from the house and was located in a ravine forty feet deep and sixty feet across. The lake was another thousand yards down the hill behind the springs. The entire area was surveyed and excavated at one point by the University of Texas as a Native American refuge, where the remains of at least a half dozen Native American bodies were exhumed.

On that particular night I stepped out to enjoy the grandeur of the universe; and while I was outside observing the stars and my spectacular view of the moon, I noticed an enthralling glow coming from the direction of the springs. I made my way from the house over to the wood-chipped path which led directly to the springs. When I reached the slope that led down to the springs, I could see that the glow was actually a fire which seemed to be fluorescent and almost translucent, with a bluish-white color emanating upwardly from its center. Everything I saw after that had the same translucent appearance.

Just at the moment I noticed it was actually a fire, I had to stop in my tracks, because I could see two Native Americans positioned approximately twenty-five feet up each of the two trees adjacent to the trail. They were dressed in full native clothing—each of them wore leather boots, leather pants, and had several feathers placed within his hair. They weren't wearing full headdress feathers, but I could distinctly see the feathers protruding from their long black hair on their heads.

Each tree was on each side of what now resembled a campsite, and by then I could also see another group of eight spirits of the Native Americans sitting around the campfire, and another three who stood between the fire and me. I saw the eldest man sitting and wearing a full headdress and several women with children close to him. I noticed all their behavior change as I approached their campsite—they seemed to take the offensive as I drew closer. As they noticed me, I think they may have perceived me as a threat and were simply protecting their community and environment. At that point I realized the energy I was sensing must be the spirits of the Native Americans who called the place home for many years, and who possibly still resided there. The experience of that community's spiritual energy imprint helped me to better understand spirits and their emotional ties to specific locations. The experience lasted for half an hour, and taught me more about the spiritual connections that we have to each other, and also to other locations. It also helped me to gain an important aspect of spirituality in a visual form, thus giving me a better understanding that we do continue to exist as a spiritual form upon leaving the material world. I could not explain why those afterlife spirits were in that specific location, but I made note of its beauty and truly enjoyed the observation.

Identifying energy forms

Another specific instance of when I directly experienced another spiritual form and its energy imprint happened late one night while I was at home, alone. I had been up late watching a television program and was lying on my couch, unwinding from a long day. I heard a noise coming from the kitchen, which was the next room over. The noise was similar to the noise a person makes when he is heavily stomping his feet as he walks about. I did not know who it was or what was happening, but I could then hear the sound of someone approaching the living room. I honestly thought someone had broken in. The steps grew louder as they sped closer, and just as the encounter reached its climax, I sat up quickly and screamed out,

"Who's there?"

The spirit then ran straight towards the front wall and out the window of the living room. I was startled. I did not get a reply or actually see the spirit, but I felt it and heard it. This particular encounter began to grow my perspective of the different forms spiritual energy may have, and what and how to identify them. Since I first noticed spiritual energy imprints, I noticed that seeing and hearing them was partially related to empathy and partially to keen observations and spiritual insight.

Sensing emotional energy

Another form of energy I came to recognize by its imprints was in direct relation to our emotions. I could physically sense certain emotions upon entering any place in which a fervent emotional occurrence had transpired. One of the earliest instances I can recall was during a visit to a close friend's home. For the first time, I could emotionally sense and experience each action and moment which had transpired there earlier. At the time I could not quite fully understand what the sensation was, or even why I was having it, but I just knew that I was moving in many different directions because of the moment-by-moment replay of emotions I felt in that location. When I spoke to my friend about it, he confirmed that everything I was experiencing mimicked what had happened there earlier that week. I later recalled and studied the feelings and sensations of the emotional energy that my friend had left in that moment at his place in space, in order to better allow myself the opportunity to understand how to recognize it again when I came across other types of emotional experiences. I reference emotion and our empathic connections to each moment because there are certain signatures of emotional energy that are sometimes louder than others, and there are also many with visible characteristics which, if carefully observed and sought, are clearly recognizable everywhere.

Sharing energy's signatures

I recall one special night as I lay in bed and meditated and focused on the moment in my normal manner; I could sense something different in the way each minute was transpiring. I knew instinctively something extraordinary was about to happen. I could physically feel a tingling sensation inside of me, and I was encountering each fervid moment coming to me in a different way than before. I focused more intently and meditated more deeply, and within an hour of obtaining a heightened state of prophetic awareness, I somehow began to feel extremely disoriented and confused. I began to experience large amounts of fear, pain, and suffering. Literally, I felt as if walls were crumbling and falling down all around and on top of me. I could see people running, crying, and screaming for their lives. I had never before felt anything like it. I could feel so much pain, sorrow, and confusion that I could not make sense of it. I recall feeling as if I were in an earthquake and was directly experiencing the panic and all the fear and disorientation that accompany one during and after an earthquake experience. It took me several hours to reach the point where I could relax and catch my breath, after which I calmed down and fell sleep. When I awoke the next morning, I learned of a devastating, 8.8-magnitude earthquake that had struck Central Chile. I was speechless when I realized I had felt the earthquake's energy signature, while it was actually happening, from over three thousand miles away. Then something important came to mind that helped to put the experience into perspective, and that was that each of our emotions carries a distinct echo.

Because of studying many of those types of experiences, I am now able to sense energy in just about any form, in any place, and at any time. It is always possible because of the energy signature that everything produces, and also because of its ability to echo.

Bringing peace to emotional disorder

There is another side to being able to sense the energy and echo signatures of something (or anything) in a supernatural or spiritual way, and that has to do with differentiating between the phenomena being interpreted. Sometimes the energy imprints reveal pain and suffering which were initially difficult for me to endure. There have been many instances when I've experienced difficult and momentarily painful emotional events as if I had been there in person, or even as if I had been the one producing the energy signature myself, when in fact I was sensing its energy from far away. I believe it's because of the sensitive empathic connection I have to everything. After many more months of participating in trying moments, I found they were becoming mentally, physically, spiritually, and emotionally draining, and sometimes difficult to understand. I began to search for better ways and techniques to control this energy and to keep myself calm when those moments occurred (which appeared to be daily).

Chakras

Specific trying emotions—such as anger, fear, confusion, or pain—are trying and aggressive in nature, and when experiencing those emotional feelings as they would occur in others was when I would become weary. I knew something was needed to assist me with the necessary adjustment to my personal emotional state. I began to study myself more closely, and when those concentrated moments of energy arrived, I noticed my palms would heat up at the same time as when my heightened state of awareness would peak, so I began searching for the energy patterns in my physical self. That was when I first found truthful information on chakras, and it seemed that the more I began to understand the energy of chakras— where they were located on my body and how they helped my body to function—the more I found certain energy patterns and abilities come to light within me. When I first noticed their distinct energy locations on my body, I could tell that they traveled in a straight line along my body's torso, beginning at my groin and rising upward above my head. I found that the first chakra is located at the groin area and called the base or root chakra, while the second is located in the abdomen and is called the sacral chakra; the third, the solar plexus chakra, is located at the center of the torso; the forth is located in the center of the chest and is called the heart chakra; the fifth, the throat chakra, is located at the esophagus; and the sixth is located in the center of forehead and is called the third eye chakra; the seventh, the crown chakra, is located on top of the head. Surprisingly, I noticed our chakras also rise slightly above our bodies for nearly another foot in a spiritual way; acting the same as the chakra points on our physical bodies. What was surprising to me was that upon first noticing their locations, I could actually physically feel the resonance and spin of their energy rising outwardly from each of their energy locations; as I passed my hands over and across each chakra energy point it felt warm and caused a slight tingle on my palms.

Chakras' behavior

I began to notice that sometimes while in a heightened state of awareness, my chakras could spin at different speeds while the palms of my hands would heat up. It was while in that higher state that I could feel some of my chakras move even more radically than some of the others. This would happen any time any moments of doubt, fear, anxiety, pain, or unpleasant states occurred, I noticed a distinct change in the chakras' spin and behavior. I could spiritually and physically feel them rotating in a different way altogether, either faster or slower, and periodically out of sync from the others. It was this observance that helped me to realize that both positive and negative emotions are interpretable partially because of the effects they have on our spirit through our chakras.

I believe this is how our positive emotions are transferred to those around us, and also how our negative emotions can also upset others spiritually. I specifically found that those thoughtful and emotional points of energy on our bodies directly contribute to our interpretations of others' feelings—we can often instantly feel when something is wrong or bothering another person. It was also because of those observations that I began to understand what was necessary to calm myself by utilizing mantra breathing techniques and focused mediation, and I found they could directly affect and alter the spin of my chakras.

Aligning chakras

Now, when those feelings became overwhelming and my senses seemed to be put on overload, I would begin to focus on my breath and meditate on each point of energy, each chakra. I found that each point located on my body was associated with specific emotions and thoughts, and when I would simply align my body's spiritual energy with my emotions, psyche, and thoughts, I could calm down from any trying emotion almost instantly. The centering technique I found must be a technique that has been here since the beginning of all our existence, because it all seemed so natural and instinctive.

I would place one hand over the other and then place them both over the first chakra point (the groin). I'd then breathe through my nasal passage, inwardly first, and then exhale outwardly through my mouth. Each breath would last for four seconds in both directions. I noticed that when my chakra energy reached its optimal rate and its spin felt completely aligned with both my emotions and thoughts, I would feel a distinct sensation within each chakra point.

The sensation was both joyful and calming, and generally would be followed by a yawn; my ears would pop, as if the pressure had been equalized from that particular energy point directly within my spirit and out to my body. I would then slide my hands upward to the next chakra point of energy, while continually maintaining focus on the four-second breaths. I could spiritually feel when I reached the next chakra point, and then I would begin the process all over again. I could feel each chakra point beneath my heated palms and the spin associated with each location. Once again, upon remaining focused on my breath and after reaching the optimal spin associated with the next spiritual chakra point, my ears would pop and I would open my mouth, letting out an enormous yawn. My body would then reach a deeper level of peace from the alignment. I continued to repeat the process and exercise as I moved upward, remaining focused on my breath from chakra point to chakra point and, to my amazement, I noticed that by the time I had reached the top chakra energy point, I was spiritually aligned and perfectly centered. At that point I gave off the deepest yawn of all, and that was generally followed by several tears. The tears themselves would subside within minutes, but the complete feeling of peacefulness and tranquility would stay long afterward. I would slowly raise my arms up over my head and then slowly place my hands alongside my body, and it was there in that moment of tranquility that I would attain all the insights from within a peaceful state of Zen. After learning of that technique I was now able to center myself and adjust to any trying emotion or situations simply by focus. Chakras have a great significance in our bodies, and I believe with proper meditation and focus they can help us all to get and stay spiritually balanced and centered in every moment.

Healing techniques

I found some other abilities were coming to light also. I realized that within a heightened state of awareness I could sense where certain places on my body were uncomfortable or out of sync; with a focused touch of my hand the pain would vanish and the painful place in question would release all its tension and return to health. I discovered this touch technique worked on muscles, tendons, and even on discs. I believe that both my heated palms and my body's centeredness contributed directly to sensing that ability and dispensing the pain. The healing attributes I felt were immediately noticeable on my shoulders, in the straightening of my back, in the range in motion of my entire body, and in the flexibility of my limbs. I had the complete removal of any pain that I previously associated with any of those places. I then noticed that although I had not taken any yoga classes or studied any of the techniques associated with yoga, I was practicing many of its stretching positions simply because it felt natural. I also found that when meditating and applying breathing techniques and while remaining centered and focused on my surroundings, I saw for the first time what is referred to as a vortex and the energy signatures that are associated with one.

Vortices

The vortices were generally accompanied with a couple of distinct energy signatures. An important aspect to keep in mind is that my observations were made with the naked eye. When it first began in my room, I had meditated for several hours and achieved a higher state of awareness. I was completely focused on the moment, and while preparing myself for all observations yet to come, out of the periphery of my right eye I noticed a brilliant and bright light. The room was still and dark, but there was a distinct sound coming from the area where the light had appeared. It sounded as if a positively charged cable had touched something grounded. The sound was distinct and when I looked over, I saw bright sparks like those of a holiday sparkler filling the immediate area. The sparks were white and star shaped. All the action seemed to be coming from the top corner of the ceiling in an area no larger than the tip of my thumb. What I didn't understand at the time was that this was the first time my mind, body, and spirit had reached the proper vibration or frequency that allowed for these observations.

That event lasted for around thirty more seconds and stopped abruptly. As I stood up to get a closer look, I saw something else puzzling coming in the opposite direction from near the base of my door (five feet away). Suddenly I could see it was a vortex.[26] It was rolling, twisting and swirling directly towards me and then I made its shape out in full. It appeared to be closing in on itself again and again, just as a vortex does. It appeared perhaps two inches in diameter and had a bluish-white color. It had little wavy lines that wrapped around each symmetrical line that swirled in on itself while it opened into a temporal nexus.[27] The vortex headed straight for me until it connected with the direct center of my forehead (my third eye chakra). At that point I could not see any end or beginning; it was a true vortex. My ears began to ring and the entire connection and wondrous moment lasted for several more seconds, twenty seconds in total. My initial reaction was one of confusion and fear. I had just experienced something so intense and unknown I didn't know how to

---

26   Vortex: A whirling mass of something, especially water or air, that draws everything near it toward its center; a situation or feeling that seems to swamp or engulf everything else
27   Nexus: A connection or link associating two or more people or things; the center or focus of something

react. I immediately felt light-headed and sat back down on my bed to contemplate what I had just seen, and what its purpose was.

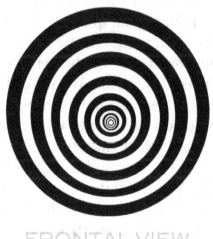

FRONTAL VIEW

I had been seeing something traveling at great speeds around me for some time already, but I couldn't quite tell what it was. I'd noticed it had an energy signature I did not recognize, but I also noticed a few constants: the phenomenon appeared to be unbound (according to our understanding of space and time), and there was also a distinct faint sound made when interactions with such a phenomena occurred, one comparable to a distinct pop from one solid object connecting to another. Whatever the sound was, I had a feeling it had to do with the arrival and departure of whatever that vortex was for. As I studied the vortices, I kept on noting that the fast-moving blurs were everywhere, and when the phenomenon occurred, my shoulders would sometimes quiver and I'd often get goose bumps. I wondered for what reason this phenomenon had been occurring and I made note of each instance and continued.

Emotional interactions

I thought it necessary to focus more on my chakras, since they had led to my centering of self, which then led to the observation of vortices. I noticed that when I was in a happy or good mood, my chakras and the chakras in those around me were able to communicate and interpret my emotional state of being. I likened it to having another way to communicate with someone without saying a word or making a gesture. I also noted that when I was in a bad or negative mood it could directly be transferable to another in the exact same manner. I determined that our emotions are directly interpretable and directly linked to everyone. The occurrences intrigued me to the point of conclusion.

I found that at all times our chakras release positive or negative energy, which directly impacts those around us and affects their emotional well-being. When a person is in a great mood, their mood can seemingly spread to others in the immediate area without any verbal communication. In a similar manner, a person who is fighting with someone, or disrupting an area, can affect others with their aggressive emotions simply by being aggressive. Their aggression is spread spiritually through their chakras and affects other people through their chakras' energy points. I also found that if not properly and immediately resolved, this connection (via our chakras) can contribute to another's aggressive, negative, or even offensive emotional nature simply by being there or observing them. I interpreted and closely observed that type of communication often, and there were even times when an aggressive nature became somewhat confusing to me—I couldn't momentarily decipher between whose energy I was actually feeling at its moment of inception. I thought that was possibly due to the aggressive nature of that type of emotional energy.

I found that when all of our chakras or energy points are in perfect alignment (or spinning properly) their spin rate and good vibrations indicate to others, mostly unbeknownst to them, that we are in a perfect state of bliss/being. Most people connect with that positive energy and are then able to share in our great mood. The sensations happen in fractions of seconds as one enters each moment. Once again, the experience of the energy being released is typically unbeknownst to the receiver, and we both send and receive at the same time.

When our emotions change from good to bad, our chakras and energy signatures all begin to resonate in another distinctive way. The important message here, I believe, is to always stay focused, centered, and aligned (if possible). If not, then recognizing the change and resolving the issue through focus, meditation, and/or centering of one's chakras (with the centering technique I've described) will always help one to get realigned. Maintaining a centeredness and balance of one's own energy should be at the forefront of all our actions, and I believe it can help us all to acquire peacefulness and acquire a state of bliss that allows for complete harmony within our bodies and with each other. I also believe that if we could perhaps learn to grasp the importance of balance and maintain our alignments of our own energy, we could acquire a path to total peace and complete harmony (a path that I believe could help all who may not currently recognize the importance of our interactions with each other).

Listening to The Winds

After having studied many philosophers with regard to the conscious and the subconscious, I had hopes of ascertaining a better understanding of reality and our perceptions of it. During my early studies I learned more of metaphysics and of its findings of the essence of the initial causes of things. I sought diligently the underlying attributes of existence and its ultimate nature. It was with that insight that I turned my drive in the direction of the motion of sound and its intrinsic energy signatures.

I can remember always being able to communicate in some way, shape or form. Expression came easily for me, and being able to understand and notice distinct attributes seemed easy as well. It was during my studies of sound that I found that, emotionally speaking, we interact in much more detail than I had previously thought; I found that our thoughts and our actions carry distinct energy signatures that echo and reverberate, which in turn directly affect those in the immediate vicinity of the sound itself. Even if the sound itself is not of an audible attribute, such as speech, the sound of our thoughts and emotions carries weight. Throughout my life I have been fortunate and blessed to be able to remember many details about many topics, subjects, and personal experiences—a blessing I'm truly thankful for. I've been able to use that ability to recollect sound and analyze it from the position of a psychic using clairvoyant attributes with transcendent ability.

As that ability first began to occur within my life, I noticed a distinct whisper that appeared to come from within my inner ear. It was the whisper coming from the being that appeared to witness and observe my every action. I couldn't quite understand what was being whispered, initially; it was brief and not always comprehensible. I noticed it would typically happen around thoughtful moments and heartfelt emotions. The whisper would generally come to me in the form of telepathy and would often seem as if it were coming from a being right next to me. It was always delivered the same, though, always in the form of a whisper. It is what many have deemed as our conscious or our inner voice. I bring this to attention because as my curiosity grew in the study of sound, I discovered (and I mentioned this earlier) that each of our thoughts and emotions carry a distinct energy imprint within its own distinctive echo which reverberates ever so subtly. Hearing it allowed me to gain more insight into sound. It also allowed me to hear that which is sometimes inaudible for some, but is absolutely there.

"So then faith comes by hearing, and hearing by the word of God." (Romans 10:17).

I compare such an ability, which I now know we all possess, to a labyrinth. When you first notice its structure every passage appears to look the same as every passage you may have ever seen before. I used to interpret and acknowledge every sound that way, but when I carefully scrutinized my observations, I found that the echoes of my thoughts reverberated off my immediate surroundings, especially when other people were near. I noticed that the perceptions we have of any assembly of others helped lead to the actual observation and interpretation of the occurrence. What I also found amazing was that even when no others were present, my thoughts still seemed to reverberate off objects with distinct signatures and echoes, and they were still distinguishable. The intricacies of the echoes of energy are amazing, and when factoring in such complexities as emotional thought, free will, and the direction of any given conversation; or when more than one conversation is apparent, being able to interpret the echo signature became incredibly relative.

When that ability initially began for me, I had an experience with a group of people that helped to open my eyes in such a way that my inner perceptions and interpretations were opened as well. I had recently had a near death experience that had partially changed my viewpoint of the material world. I mention near death moments because I have had many of them throughout my life, beginning at the age of three.

My first near death experience

The first encounter I had with a near death experience, I was three and traveling to the grocery store with my dad. He sat me in the front seat of the car and put the seatbelt over me. Things were different back then, it was okay to put your child in the front seat, and besides we were just going to the store a few blocks away. We had just left our house, and as we turned off of our street, the car door opened and I slid out from under the seatbelt and fell out of the car. We weren't traveling at a very fast speed; however, it was fast enough for me to hit the road at about twenty miles an hour and roll over myself several times before I began to scream and cry. It was that very instance that changed my life. I have always had insight, but in that moment I saw and felt an experience that I recognize now as an NDE (near death experience). I have had many NDEs in my life, ten I believe, with each one shedding more insights into what truly happens when moments like those come to fruition.

Each near death experience significantly affected my life in many ways. Many may never completely understand or experience one firsthand, and although I have been fortunate enough to still be here in this amazing world, there were many instances when I wasn't sure if I would make it. What amazed me most is that with each encounter and recovery, distinct otherworldly insights became visible.

There was one particular event that I contribute directly to my being able to hear and decipher the whisper I've just described. I had come close to death during a family gathering, and had it not been for the help of several family members, I might not have survived. The exact moment it happened, many otherworldly abilities came to light, and hearing was one of them. It took several days to recover from that incident, but when I did, the world was completely different. Something miraculous had occurred within, and I had developed a deeper level of spiritual discernment to all moments. I could see and hear in a way unlike before which in turn opened the door to many supernatural insights.

Whispers in the wind

That was when I began to understand what it truly means to listen to the wind. When I listen to the winds, I listen to the natural sounds of the earth. Everything in God's creation has its own distinct energy signature, and when I pay careful attention to the natural sounds of life, I found even thoughts became recognizable. The thoughts, ever so subtle and soft, are undoubtedly there. That was around the same time that I began to hear the unique whisper (which helped me to recognize and even interpret certain sounds of moments, events, actions, emotions, and thoughts of my own and from others). It also gave way to intrinsic insights into current moments and moments yet to come.

One of the first times the echo of my thoughts stood out, I had fasted for several days, meditated, and centered myself in order to prepare for the highest order of truth (a truth that presents itself like no other and gives way to life-changing moments of insight). One evening, some friends and I had gathered to celebrate another friend's birthday, and we were ready to be entertained by a band in the backyard of his house. We were all served food and drinks while we listened to the band. There were over thirty friends and guests present, and I noticed we all let to the moment and became emotionally synced. When we became emotionally synced I was able to gain insight into this particular perception.

The house was decorated with many lights, both inside and out, and there were at least four different families present with their kids playing about. The atmosphere felt electrically charged; I noticed something different. Something distinct was in the air—a type of environment, I realize now, that happens around moments such as those. We congregated in the backyard while the musicians began to tune their instruments. The three musicians—a vocalist who played the acoustic guitar, an electric guitar player, and the young man on a drum box—had not played publicly before. The energy of the band, coupled with the good vibrations, set the stage for my ability to interpret and witness how our thoughts and emotions echo in an emotional, personal, and social gathering.

I began to notice that when any given moment to come would give me a truly joyful feeling, that joyfulness would help me to better sense and to hear the entire social moment in a very unique way. It allowed me to fully understand a single moment of the immediate future. That held true, but for only a fraction of a second or so. The truth of the moment to come would transpire briefly before the actual moments would occur. If I heard the moment which was to come in the form of a slight whisper, I could then analyze the whisper as if I had mentally recorded it. I could mentally play it forward and backward in any direction. In my mind I compare it to having a recorded audio segment and having the ability to move about the recording at will within the few milliseconds of the voice having whispered.

It was while learning of that ability that I began to understand how to walk into a crowded room and make an instant recording of everyone who was conversing within the moment. I could clearly make out what was being said throughout the entire gathering. Whether a conversation was in direct regard to me or not, I could maneuver through each sound almost instantly and simultaneously. When the occurrence first began to reveal insights, I had to practice deciphering what I was hearing. I would compare it to learning my ABCs all over again or perhaps to learning how to read using phonics. I had to sound out the letters and interpret by comparison. I was, for the first time, learning the transcendence of sound and how to navigate it.

Echo signatures

I was soon able to determine that the whisper I was hearing also included my thoughts. I would hear a whisper and then I would have a thought. As I analyzed the sound of the whisper, I then realized the whisper was the thought I would have immediately following it. I was intrigued. I needed to better understand how this process works.

I realized at that point that all of our thoughts have an echo signature that is just as noticeably audible as any other sound I had been interpreting. I recognized this was possible partially because of this first thought's inception and at the time it was sounded out by others in my direct vicinity. Incredibly I thought *This is a great event,* and I immediately noticed the sound of my thought in the conversations which were transpiring all around me. It was very similar in movement to the signatures of energy waves. Although the exact words "This is a great event" did not come directly from one person's mouth, the sentence was actually broken up and uttered between several people within several groups close by. One person said "This" while another said "is a"; another said "great," and then I heard "event" from someone else. The entire experience transpired immediately after I had the thought. It was such a surprising experience to witness. I knew it could be considered coincidence, but seeing as I don't believe in coincidence and I had noticed that phenomenon again and again, I knew it was a truth that had always existed. That one moment helped to me to realize just how significant all of our thoughts are and just how sensitive we actually are to all others' thoughts. At that point I began researching and studying more and more about that type of energy, its echo signature, and how and why it's possible.

I studied whispers for a long period of time, noticing the moments when the whisper from the past led to a thought in the present that echoed in the future. I also noticed that when I didn't quite hear or understand what was being whispered, I would sometimes get a response. I know how this may appear or read, however, I did not verbally carry on a conversation with another person physically next to me. As I mentioned before, the first time I ever noticed the presence of another being was during a relative out-of-body perspective. I came to understand that that and similar types of experiences were what one may call clairvoyant, clairaudient, or even supernatural.

The more often I practiced reaching a higher state of awareness (through meditation, breathing techniques, aligning of my chakras, positioning of my proper consciousness with positive emotions, all encompassed by faith and penitence), the more conversational the whisper became, and I knew it was directly related to the fast-traveling phenomenon that left its energy signatures in every emotional and thoughtful moment I had.

The presence

I lay in bed with the lights off one night (as I would normally do while meditating, focusing, and in search of greater understanding in regards to everything everywhere), when I noticed I could physically sense the presence of another being. It was comparable to the sense of someone walking into my room. The knob had not been turned, nor had the door been pressed and pushed opened, yet I could tell I was not alone. I could literally see, in the dark, that certain attributes and features were becoming noticeable. Something kept coming in and out of the room at will, and it seemed to be tied directly to my emotions and thoughts. I would periodically stare up towards the corner of the ceiling where I had first seen bright sparks, and over a short period of time I began to clearly see an energy force whose vitality seemed to contradict my previous understanding of matter and energy and our relationships between them.

I knew there had to be some sort of spiritual system in place that would allow for what it was that kept entering my room. I knew it must have happened for me to have seen it, and I began thinking of the entrance points and the type of energy that was coming from and going to these points. Although the lights were off, it was still somewhat visible. I could tell the location of its entry point was very small, and then I noticed that it was not set to any one area or location. I thought of what it would be like to move in such a way—from wherever its place was to here on the material plane of earth—and about how its type of movement must seem similar to the way we perceive our motion.

Entering a vortex

After lying in bed one evening and having gone through many emotions both positive and negative, I had attained a heightened state of awareness of the moment which allowed for a transitional out-of-body perspective. All of a sudden I could feel myself floating. I had focused my thoughts on traveling along this transit system of sorts and how it must feel to navigate it, when suddenly I began to enter what I know now as a vortex. It was light blue and several inches in diameter. It seems that while focused on the entranceway, I had somehow maneuvered towards it and entered. I realize now it was a temporal nexus. I then found myself traveling at great speeds. I could see the horizon split in two as I moved through and increased in velocity, and I could see myself passing between translucent clouds—with magenta and deep purple undertones—scattered both above and below me. There was light within the system that illuminated everything, though I couldn't quite tell where it was coming from.

Finally, after traveling for several minutes, I appeared to arrive at an unknown destination. There were others there that appeared to be like humans, or they at least carried very similar attributes (but with ever-so-subtle distinctions of appearance). They seemed alarmed at the fact that I was there, and then everyone saw me and left the place in a hurry. I could see I was in a large structure—a facility for some specific type of function. I saw many of these beings' sitting at workstations within a work area and their hurried movements startled me and I thought about being back in my room. I returned instantly, sat up, immediately realizing I was awake; I had not been dreaming, nor were my eyes closed. I analyzed the moment for a while, wondering how it was possible and if I could do it again, where this place was, and if what I had just experienced was part of everyone's life.

As these moments increased in frequency, I was extremely appreciative to be blessed with such encounters. I hope that these insights cause as much curiosity in others as it did in me. I believe it's naturally instinctive for us to hope to discover such a wondrous view of life or to, at the very least, hope to relate to such insights. I believe most of us hope to gain a greater perspective of another world we can't quite seem to put our finger on but are relatively aware of its existence.

I moved forward, often contemplating my thoughts on my recent experiences, questioning how and why I had sometimes witnessed quiescently beautiful moments and at other times observed raucously complex moments. I came to the conclusion that there is a reason for everything—every action, every thought, every moment—and we are all blessed with such moments in the world. I knew there was a greater purpose to all I had been witnessing, although I did not yet know what that reason was, I felt compelled to continue in hopes of gaining a greater understanding into an unknown yet wonderful experience of life.

Listening to conversation

It was soon thereafter when I overheard a conversation being held in regards to me. The conversation was extremely low in tone and volume, but I could make it out. I couldn't quite tell where, what, or who the conversation was being held by; but as the discussion grew, I could make out that it was directly related to what I had been experiencing. Next, I heard someone distinctly say,

"He's listening."

The conversation went back and forth without a sound in the natural realm. I would simply think of a question and I would get a response to it, or I would respond to what I heard. I was uncertain as to the origin of the responses and, truth be told, I was dismissive, skeptical, and even offensive. I just didn't get it right away. I didn't quite understand that what I was experiencing was otherworldly and of a divine nature.

Casting judgment

I had finally begun to accept what I was experiencing, and then I saw in great detail, for the first time, where this whisper was coming from. I was lying in bed late one evening, as I would often do. I had gone through a multitude of emotions, as I often had, and as the mental conversation centered more on truth, and learning how to pay careful attention to the moment, I caught a glimpse of the being for several moments. I don't know why, but I was even ruder than I had been before. I thought this being to a monster. I was terrified with seeing something otherworldly, something I didn't understand and had never heard of before. I simply didn't get it; I was so quick to cast judgment and give a response without realizing what I was saying or doing. My natural mannerisms had gone completely out the window, and I was treating the being I'd just seen very rudely. I had to apologize and remember I had been taught that just because I don't understand someone or something, I should not label and judge, lest I be judged or labeled myself.

"Judge not, that you be not judged." (MATTHEW 7:1).

More beings

We spoke for a few moments and this being reminded me of a blue genie. I could make out the color of its skin—and its unique spiritual appearance. It hovered several feet above me and was unique in its way. It was during that brief interaction that I was asked if it would be okay with me to have some others visit. I was not sure what that meant, but I was intrigued to see what that was all about, so I agreed to the request. The figure that had been speaking to me was much smaller than an average person—it reminded me of what I had read of a genie. This being was several feet in length, and blue.

I thought back to the first time I had noticed a supernatural being along side of me and remembered that was when I had first stepped out-of-body as to see the parameters of space and time. The supernatural being that I saw then was the same size, color and shape, and its proximity to me was very similar to the one now beside me, and so I believed the being to be one and the same.

When the other spiritual beings first began to visit, I could see that many of them had forms that united and intertwined as they constantly rolled over each other. The supernatural beings completely embraced one another for long periods of time. Most of the spiritual beings within my room seemed to move in a similar fashion around my bed. They were watching me; I was watching them. Their facial appearances would change right before my eyes—they were always in a constant state of movement yet still have the defining characteristics of what we associate with a face. Their eyes, ears, nose, and mouth would constantly change. They all had different characteristics similar to humans—height, weight, hair—all helping to differentiate one from another. They seemed intrigued with me, and they would periodically come in closer for a better look and then move away hurriedly, as if slightly apprehensive in regards to getting too close to me. They were still learning who and what I was.

The first of several of their noticeable characteristics I noticed was their skin color—I could see a deep blue, black, and a lighter shades of tan. I thought about how God is a wonderful creator and then I knew that they were of a divine nature and that I was experiencing something much greater than I understood.

More visitors arrive

For the next several months, I noticed that the spiritual beings who appeared to be in a constant state of embrace were not the only visitors I was having. There were many other spiritual beings present, only now I began to notice their visible differences. I could see that the spiritual beings that were in a constant state of embrace would seem to depart and arrive in a different manner than the other celestial beings did—they would enter each moment in an instant; an opening would appear for them which was extremely minuscule, and possibly beyond the visual capabilities of some.

The newer celestial and spiritual beings had a warm and peaceful presence to them; I felt at ease in their company, and I could see their visual characteristics amazingly clear. I noticed different variations of these supernatural beings, and the way they arrived and departed was unlike anything I had ever seen before. When they first appeared to me, I could see many tiny particles—reminiscent of the way mist forms from water—only those particles sparkled with energy, and as they shimmered and glistened they would form into an astral/spiritual body. When they reached their spiritual forms they would appear to be either male or female, yet within a matter of moments their presence would change from one gender to the other. One spot would sparkle on their bodies and that one spot would start a type of transformation. The change would begin where each sparkle or energy point glistened, and then began to move outward to encompass their entire beings in a matter of seconds. Once complete, their transformation would reveal an alternate being opposite to the one I had just seen.

There were many other spiritual beings that changed in an entirely different way than just described, and I could see that they maneuvered in a few different ways too. As I was in close proximity to all of the celestial beings, the angels, I saw one that burst back into a fine mist of energy particles from spiritual form. Then, in an instant, he followed an arched course that moved him to the other side of my room. I somehow knew those moving in such a way were archangels. I was captivated with their otherworldly exuberance. If I lost my focus for even a moment, they would not stay visible in spiritual form; they would appear to take on an outlined form reminiscent of a vivacious light-colored shadow, and when I regained my sight and focus, I could see them yet again.

Other worlds

So there I lay, surrounded by divine supernatural phenomena and hoping to gain more insight and understanding into all this, when I suddenly began to see people, places, and events I'd never seen before, all accompanied by insight. One of the first visions of another otherworldly place (which I will describe in more detail later in the book) I would describe as a large hall or vestibule where several fifty-foot-tall people ushered many smaller people through its hallways. The hallways were grand and much taller than most human structures I'd seen, with ceilings over one hundred feet high. The walls were earth tone, and light brown; and as I moved through the grand hallway I noticed a large mural, and an enormous window that was oval shaped. I gazed out through it and I could see white clouds where the ground would normally be, and blue skies above. I didn't understand where I was, but I thought it could possibly be an entrance into another realm. I would later find out the tall beings were another type of angel. This moment lasted for several minuets and then I found myself home again.

The meetings with the supernatural beings kept happening night after night for several more months, and each night was progressively more insightful than the one before. I kept observing many wondrous locations I'd not seen before—I was able to determine that these places do simultaneously exist, and they are somehow interwoven with the material world in which we live. I was completely intrigued with all I was seeing, I needed to know more though. I needed to understand exactly what was happening.

The experiences of others

I began to study more about ancient wisdom, ascension, angels, and physics. I was particularly curious about my visitors—and the hows and whys—so I looked for similar experiences of others from the past. I was searching for a way to bring all of these experiences and insights together in order to open my eyes to the limitless possibilities of every moment. I also hoped to bring further understanding of how we perceive and interact with one another. I discovered stories of individuals who claimed to have experienced seeing the supernatural and spiritual beings that appeared to be in a constant state of embrace. It was soon after finding them that the validity of some of my experiences came to light. I couldn't quite understand the significance of the visitations though, but as the miraculous insights and experiences continued, I knew there was something of great importance about to be revealed. As always, I zealously observed, noted, and moved forward with deliberate intent.

Enlightenment and Spirituality

Ever since the inception of my journey, I had been searching for peace and understanding within each moment of life, and then I was searching for focus and zeal to better process the supernatural events that seemed to transpire with what was now each breath. Although I felt great joy in my findings there seemed to be something still missing—a piece of the puzzle I'd not yet perhaps discovered, or a certain clarification ready to unfold at any moment and reveal what I truly searched for—a greater truth of the moments of life. I could feel the great truth on the horizon.

I did not know at the time, but I was in search of nirvana—not necessarily a place where one would expect to find something tangible, but more so a feeling or sensation of perfection (or as close to perfect as one may hope to attain while alive and living on earth). I was in search of the perfect condition within a state of bliss. I'd come to know how delicate a balance there is between this world and the next. My emotions and thoughts were centered delicately within that balance, and the moment-by-moment effects of my emotions, thoughts, and actions could lead to an occurrence of panic and fear or, alternatively, to an occurrence of Zen and peacefulness. The slightest misinterpretation, variation, or indecision could bring about confusion or pain, while the correct one would bring about joy. A fine line and a narrow path had truly been revealed.

Our every moment-by-moment thoughts and decisions could be seen as trivial in the material world, but I was noticing just how all our words, thoughts, and emotions made a hugely significant impact on all of our lives spiritually. Grasping that truth allowed me to better understand the balance between our two worlds and allowed me to focus on the essential aspect of peace and harmony, and so I studied two paths to further my understanding—the first being an exercise in futility and the second in humility. These two paths exist simultaneously within each of us, but seldom are we aware of their full force spiritually; and even when we are, it doesn't necessarily cause us to always walk the correct path in life.

Self-centered vs. selflessness

There are many circumstances which can cause one to lose sight of the absolute truth. I've found that during these many supernatural encounters, there were moments which taught me insightful lessons about myself spiritually. First, I noticed that when focusing on this world in a self centered manner, I could open myself up to misinterpreting my thoughts or emotions. When I misinterpreted my interactions with certain supernatural beings who intended to test, challenge, or misguide me, my self centeredness would lead to doubt, uncertainty, or fear. That sometimes led directly to panic, or frustration, which in turn could lead to anger, hatred, or violence—a path of futility.

I've found living selfless without ego and humbly living confidently is the foundation for greatness in life. This allows for one to truly find and understand the path of absolute truth. It leads to spiritual knowledge and insight which, in turn, can directly bring forth a spiritual light from within—a spiritual light that may allow for a divine union to occur.

In order to live in the perfect balance of these two ever-presents worlds:

1. We must acknowledge the balance of the material and spiritual worlds in our lives. According to the natural law of balance, without one the other may not exist. Without this spiritual awareness, we can't fully realize an enlightened state of being truly exist within. We must understand this truth in order to know what we are or are not in search of.

2. We must be humble with ourselves. Humility includes all our thoughts of ourselves and towards others, and our emotions. It guides us towards peace, understanding, harmony, bliss and, ultimately, to enlightenment.

3. In order to reach absolute truth and spiritual enlightenment we cannot live in a self-serving way. We must be completely egoless/selfless and completely fearless.

Narcissism and humility don't necessarily fall into their respective positive and negative slots, but the complete absence of the former is most definitely a necessity if one has hopes of attaining the superlative truth and of miraculously achieving enlightenment.

Searching for enlightenment

There are many steps one must make to obtain enlightenment, and there are many paths to its attainment. Each journey is sacred and must be made with an understanding of the spirit. There are no instructions, but there are underlying principles and foundations which must be followed in hopes of understanding the essence of one's true spiritual existence.

When I began, I did not understand why I was in constant search of everything. I had not considered theology, nor had I used intellectual studies or intuition to experience the perfect state of bliss I aspired to reach. I had felt the existence of such a truth long before its realization. I did not know where to begin; I simply felt and knew that I must.

I instinctively felt that meditation was one of the foundations I had to learn about in much greater depth. I had already come to understand and utilize it with effective results. Meditation was becoming a big part of the experiences I've mentioned, but it was when I had reached that pinnacle of spiritual insight and understanding of enlightenment that the meditative techniques took on a whole new meaning to me. I could feel myself and my surroundings in a whole new way; meditation had assisted me in spiritually seeing within myself and to also see myself in a spiritual form. I found that there are many ways and many reasons to meditate, and that each one should be entered and examined carefully. I searched for the essential principals of meditation utilizing empirical observations, and I was intuitively drawn towards the natural cycle of breath, which is what first led me to study mantra breathing techniques. I found that when these focused techniques were properly utilized and incorporated into my every moment, I gained a perspective I might not have had otherwise.

When I first began meditating, I'd had no previous training in the field. The techniques I began with came simply from a position I had seen others engaged in throughout my life—the lotus. As I began to practice, my eyes instinctively closed and my breath naturally deepened; my legs were comfortably crossed and I held one hand over one another across my knees, as if to facilitate the natural flow of my body's energy. At first, I began to truly observe the motion and duration of my breath—how it comes in, completes, turns in direction, moves out, and concludes. It all seemed to symbolize and represent life and death. As I would focus on my breath, all else would slowly begin to fade away. I could increase the duration of an inhalation or exhalation and instantly determine its effects on my thoughts, my relaxation state, and my emotions.

With that technique, I began to achieve a certain focus that I applied to every moment. I hoped for greater understanding of the supernatural encounters I was witnessing, and my hope was rewarded—many intrinsic truths have since been determined. It was also while practicing these focused breathing techniques that I was able to find many energy patterns, attain a heightened state of awareness, learn how to make distinctions between both inner and outer occurrences, and discover the ideal conditions of the moment that allow for complete peace and harmony within.

The spirit world

I decided to look further into monotheistic religions, and began by examining my past. I found that my mother's grandfather, my great grandfather, was a full-blooded Native American, so I decided to research Native American spiritual beliefs and practices. I wanted to better understand what is sometimes referred to as the spirit world by the Native Americans. I found that shamans are said to be holy people who had many functions within the early Native American community.[28] Most importantly, they helped to guide and protect their people, give direction, and further their own understanding with meditation and ancient rituals specifically designed to merge with nature. Some had the ability to foretell future events, and to know and utilize clairvoyant and psychic abilities. Based on what I learned of early shamanism, I began seeking more visions and a better understanding of spirits and the spirit world.

As those abilities became more recognizable within, I could hear the voices of those close to me while in a focused state of awareness. I would sometimes have visions of future courses of important events, or of relationships of those close to me, or of my path and my future. I would later realize that the voices and visions would often reveal what was in my heart, and in the hearts of others close to me or those thinking of me.

Examining religions

As I continued my journey, I examined all religion more closely (Catholicism was the religion I had grown up with).[29] It is said that to be Catholic is to be universal in extent, character, and application. My faith in God had always been strong and true, but I found more and more topics which were quickly dismissed by Catholicism as heresy.[30] I found beliefs that were limited and were directly

28   Shaman: A spiritual leader who is believed to have special powers such as prophecy and the ability to heal
29   Catholicism: A broad term for the body of the Catholic faith, its theologies and doctrines, its liturgical, ethical, spiritual, and behavioral characteristic
30   Heresy: An opinion or belief that contradicts established religious teaching

contributing to my fear (for a lack of understanding). I found there were some questions the Catholic Church simply could not answer. My immediate response to the new encounters was fear. I could see that the fear was caused by something that I didn't understand. I thought that the experiences I was beginning to have weren't of God—an opinion and practice that I understand now was from a lack of understanding that all things have come from God. Within my experience I learned that there is no room for fear. I strongly feel that when any religion (and I speak of Catholicism first because of being familiar with its practices) does not fully meet every spiritual need in a person, then it should not dismiss or misguide the seeker in his/her need for proper guidance and a better understanding of God. I found that God has created everything everywhere and is above all things; he is all and in all. I just didn't fully understand at the time that this universal truth is completely woven into every part of all our lives. I believe, however, in the Church and of its importance in providing us with a place to worship God, and to come together and help one another find God. I believe in the power of prayer and its ability to move mountains, and I believe in organized religion and its ability to help those who are in need or in search of God. I also believe that we should all be mindful of what we are learning and how we apply our wisdom towards each other and toward the world.

Different studies

I studied more about different religions including Buddhism, Hinduism, Judaism, Daoism, Confucianism, Jainism, Baha'i, Sikhism, and Islam; and all the different forms of spirituality like Mysticism, Sufism, and Kabbalah, all from the viewpoint of a theologian looking for understanding and spiritual insight of what he had learned.[31,32,33,34,35,36,37,38,39,40,41,42] I had hoped to read direct descriptions by others who had experienced what I was undergoing daily. To my amazement, I found many similarities within these religions—most had the superlative belief that there is only one God and only one path to find God. I was astonished to learn that as divine and diverse as the world is, and as different as we are from one another and from country to country, all religions share the notion that there is only one correct way to God and that all others must be delusional and their followers wasting their prayers. I was completely amazed at how any one religion can claim to be the only right path that leads to God. I believed and learned that all good paths lead to God.

There are many forms of spirituality, for the most part originally derived from each of the monotheistic religions

31   Buddhism: Based on the teaching of the Buddha and holding that a state of enlightenment can be attained by suppressing worldly desires
32   Hinduism: Characterized by a belief in reincarnation and a large pantheon of gods and goddesses
33   In Judaism, God is the creator of everything and the source of all goodness
34   Daoism: One of the two great indigenous philosophical traditions of China.
35   Confucianism: The belief that personal communication or union with the divine is achieved through intuition, faith, ecstasy, or sudden insight rather than through rational thought
36   Jainism: An ancient branch of Hinduism that rejects the notion of a supreme being and advocates a deep respect for all living things
37   Baha'i: A religion founded in Iran in 1863 that maintains that the teachings of all religions are of value and humankind is spiritually one, and advocates world peace
38   Sikhism: A religious group that broke away from Hinduism during the 16th century and advocated a monotheistic doctrine, incorporating some aspects of Islam
39   Islam: A monotheistic religion based on the word of God as revealed to Muhammad during the 7th century
40   Mysticism: The belief that personal communication or union with the divine is achieved through intuition, faith, ecstasy, or sudden insight rather than through rational thought
41   Sufism: Muslim mysticism
42   Kabbalah: A body of mystical Jewish teachings based on an interpretation of the Hebrew scriptures as containing hidden meanings

I studied, but each one also developed different sects based on its beliefs and practices. I could understand how developing and practicing orthodox spiritual rituals could help one continue on one's path, but I was having difficulty understanding why some spiritual practices were excluded or unrecognized. So I looked more closely at the reasons for exclusions and at the unorthodox practices and why they were dropped or overlooked.

An unbiased conversation

I hadn't quite completed my inquiries into the different monotheistic religions when one evening, while meditating, I heard a familiar whisper that seem to quietly come from nearby. I communicated back and forth with the celestial being (through my thoughts), and the conversation seemed to steer towards religion and denominations—a sensitive topic of discussion for most. Surprisingly, the conversation stayed unbiased and did not sway. People tend to steer a conversation towards understandings their own views, beliefs, and practices whether they are practitioners of that religion or not. The conversation began to reveal to me that I carried and practiced all the different forms of spirituality simultaneously (see list in previous footnotes).

Understanding my self as an enlightened spiritual man of God first meant understanding that the path on which I was walking seemed to be slightly different than many of those of who I knew and of those of who I had studied. It also meant that I had to learn to incorporate the many beautiful beliefs and understandings together so that I might take my next step towards a greater overall spiritual perspective. I understood that using mantra breathing exercises was considered a spiritual practice of Hinduism, but the same breathing practices used in Hinduism were related and utilized in the Christian practice of mysticism.

My enlightened viewpoint of the world and my study of the Mandala gave me spiritual insight into the Buddhist aspect of spirituality, while I prayed and utilized the Christian, Buddhist, Hindu, Taoist, and Judaistic customs and beliefs in prayers.[43,44,45] I added exercise—mental, spiritual, and physical (including yoga and the alignment of my chakras). I included the Native American aspect of spirituality into my viewpoint of the earth and every sacred part of the land. Like Kabbalah, the tree of life became my guiding symbol while on my journey. I learned that the philosophy and practice of Jainism emphasized the necessity of self-effort to move the soul towards divine consciousness and liberation, a practice I'd also begun to incorporate into every view of life. After looking into the Baha'i faith with my viewpoint of spirituality, I understood my view was also the same—I, too, was hoping for the unification of all on earth. I would often motion to others as they approached saying hello and goodbye the way Native Americans would with the pass of my hand. I would also often speak the greetings of Islam, As-Salaam-Alaikum, which means peace—peace be to you or unto you—simply because it made me feel good inside knowing that I was hoping peace to others. Finally, I learned the Sikh method of seeking to understand and experience God, a practice I found myself in every day.

I believed in and combined all the practices in hopes of finding the ultimate truth, which I know and understand to be God. It was with these many religious and spiritual

---

43   Tantric: A movement in Hinduism and Buddhism, especially a variety based on yoga and intended to release energy through sexual intercourse in which the orgasm is withheld or delayed
44   Mandalas: In Buddhism and Hinduism, a geometric or pictorial design usually enclosed in a circle, representing the entire universe and used in meditation and ritual
45   Tao: In Taoist philosophy, the order and wisdom of individual life, and the way that this harmonizes with the universe as a whole

understandings that I could truly begin to see the truth flourishing all around me.

Theology

My goal was to study and incorporate all the different types of the known spiritualities in order to better understand the monotheistic religions, and this included the study of the nature of God and of religious truths—theology. I found that each religion is a consequence of a set of beliefs; all holding their own sacred rituals and practices accordingly, and all of them aspiring to lead their believers to God. It is a truth that I had always believed in, always known, and always felt. I began to see and feel God's presence in everything everywhere. I could see that my prayers were becoming more conversational, and that although our reality is here in the material world, my understanding and perspective of the spiritual world was becoming more interwoven with this material world.

The next study was of the spirituality of Christianity, what is often referred to as Mysticism. Its practices go beyond the mainstream of most practicing Christians. They include breathing exercises (similar to the mantra techniques I had been learning and applying daily), deeper levels of spiritual discernment, and prayer. I incorporated all in hopes of gaining insights into a heightened state of awareness—qualities and attributes I would deem necessary for all who are worshipful and earnestly devout. They were practices that helped me to gain core perceptions of many aspects of my sacred journey. All these beliefs and practices are in the world and have been utilized to bring a greater understanding of who we are in the grand scheme of all things.

Religious practices

I then began to look further into what would transpire as I would practice traditional and long-established beliefs and what would happen by not practicing them. I hoped to understand how they affected me. What I found was that there were many different practices which are important aspects of each religious and spiritual belief and I found their beliefs and practices were established to either give a greater meaning on how to worship God, or how to be in that religion. I found many beliefs and customs practiced by many different religious and spiritual sects to bring one closer to God but strangely enough, I could not find one occurrence of all those beliefs and practices being combined. What I found was that there was no harm associated with adding or even combining other religious or spiritual practices to give an even greater scope of spirituality and of religion.

I found that for me by practicing and combining all the different spiritualities, I was able to reach the deeper levels of spiritual discernment I had hoped to attain. I could see that each of the different sects of Christianity I studied had developed its own spiritual practices and beliefs, and each one then chose to either add or remove practices—often longstanding spiritual beliefs or those associated with another perspective of spirituality simply because they felt it was not the right way to worship God. In studying all the religious Christian sects, I could feel the truth of the essential principles of spirituality; I could sense their origins ever so closely; I could sense God. I questioned that if the entire wealth of spiritual practices and beliefs were combined into one and practiced, wouldn't we all become spiritually complete?

Mysticism and spiritualism

I was beginning to understand the quality or state of being concerned with religion or religious matters, the quality or state of being spiritual. I found truth in two important aspects of mystical spirituality. Mysticism, I found was described as a practice that sought union with the divine through meditation and contemplation. I understood it as experiencing inherent thoughts and insights into divine knowledge, thoughts which give clarity into every aspect of life, both here and beyond. Being mystical (or experiencing such a spiritual connection) helped shed new light on the experiences I had witnessed and now become a part of. I realized that the conversations I'd been having had led me to my inquiry of spirituality, which helped me better understand that I am also a spiritualist.[46] My understanding of a spiritualist is that he/she is one who believes in supernatural events relating to sacred things (of the spirit, i.e. supernatural beings/angels). I found that the dictionary definition of spiritualism, however, is that it is belief in communication with the dead.

I found that a clairvoyant/clairaudient metaphysician who utilizes empirical observations and psychic abilities in search of truth, who is also rooted in virtue, can communicate with and see spirits; but he/she can also see and commune with supernatural beings, spirits, and angels.[47,48] I bring that to attention because as my interpretations began to reveal more insights into what I was experiencing, I realized I had been visited by many spirits in many places. I had often seen them, heard them, and directly felt them; I hadn't realized just how many

46   Spiritualist: One who believes that the dead can make contact with the living through the person of a medium
47   Clairvoyant: Somebody who is supposedly able to perceive things that are usually beyond the range of human senses
48   Metaphysician: A scholar who specializes in the branch of philosophy concerned with the study of the nature of being, existence, time and space, and causality

times until spirituality became an integral part of my life. I was finally able to completely grasp the concept that the whisper I had been long hearing was often coming from a supernatural and celestial being—from an angel.

Proof

I was thinking back to when I was first told of being in God's grace when I heard a whisper and an enlightening conversation commenced. The meeting centered on my actions and decisions and it carried on for what appeared to be hours. I had a thought regarding how many people in the world were looking for proof of what I had often been experiencing. Immediately following that thought I was mentally asked,

"Do you need proof?"

I replied, "I have faith; I don't need proof."

"That's very good," I heard next, and the conversation continued and went back and forth with more inquiry into why I had been conducting myself in such an unusual manner. It was during this conversation I heard someone say,

"I've never seen anything like James before."

I wasn't quite sure what to think of that! I knew that I had been learning many different spiritual lessons and that some of these lessons were taking long periods of time to fully grasp. What did this mean? I wondered how I was different and who was this saying these things.

Yahweh

It was during an experience very similar to that encounter that I had something wonderful happen: I was experiencing many emotions and seeing signs throughout the course of the evening—empathy, clairvoyance, and clairaudience— and while I meditated and focused on my breath and practiced breathing techniques for nearly an hour, a peculiar sensation emanated from my body. I could physically sense that my chakras were out of alignment, so I focused on my ability to center myself. Upon reaching a perfect state of bliss, I felt completely calm. I had attained one of the most tranquil moments of my life. Each breath seemed rhythmic and in perfect harmony with my thoughts and my surroundings. My thoughts were as pure as was my heart, and it was at that point I realized Yahweh. I was thinking about Jesus and I was thinking about how he was crucified, and at that point the word *Yahweh* came from my mouth. I then heard another ask,

"What is the reason for you having said this?"

I replied, "I could sense God everywhere; and the word simply came to mind and I spoke it."

The conversation went back and forth for a long period of time and I heard,

"God is to the people as Yahweh is to the world."

I repeated the phrase several times to instill it in my memory. Later that morning I searched for the meaning and found that Yahweh is said to be the name of God. I felt so happy to learn that, I began to cry tears of joy. It was in this moment I was told of a great many things that would come to pass. I was told I would some day become a spiritual leader and then I was asked how I would respond to those who would have questions understanding religious and spiritual truths that I would one day have.

I replied, "The line forms to the left and I would answer their questions to the best of my ability one at a time."

A new perspective

I began to understand that the conversations I had been having were with celestial beings, and that the conversations were sacred events preceding something I did not yet fully understand. My experiences were beginning to show that many of the insights I had obtained were from many angels. The beings I had seen previously had the both feminine and masculine characteristics—attributes clearly said to be angelic traits—but I hoped to gain another glimpse into a spiritual world (or worlds we know very little of) our material world seems to be directly aligned with.

I began with prayer to God. I had often prayed and asked for angels to guide and help me and my family through many tough and pleasant times. I can recall praying to the archangel Gabriel in hopes of his help to guide and assist me through my journey of life. Soon thereafter, something happened in my room.

In the forest

I recall having closed my eyes, and as soon as I blinked, three beings were standing in front of me. My surroundings had been transformed in an instant to that of another realm, an outdoor forest area, and I stood along a grass-lined path in it. The being I stood directly before carried the head and facial attributes of a lion. I believed all three beings to be cherubim.

I could see all their facial characteristics. The being behind the one directly in front of me had the head of an eagle, and the one standing behind him had the head of a man. They were all positioned in such a way that I could see their attire, their stances, and their expressions. They appeared to be dressed in armor the color of gold, which covered their torsos. The being with the head of a lion gazed directly into my eyes from merely inches away, and he began to growl as if indicating his proximity, or perhaps simply warning me to be mindful of where I was standing. In another instant, the meeting had concluded and I was back in my room.

Ascension

My interest in heaven had first peaked when I saw the place I referred to as a grand hallway, which appeared to sit on the clouds. I was not sure where that place was, but it fascinated me in such a way as to inquire into ascension and its background, and to see if it was truly possible for a man to ascend to otherworldly places while still alive. I first thought that place might be heaven, and I had read of several instances of people ascending to heaven while still alive. I began having a discussion with the archangel Gabriel about saints and others who were said to have that ability. I was curious to know about what I had been experiencing, and surprisingly, I found out there were several people, priests, friars, and saints who were said to occasionally be in two locations at the same time: bilocation. The topic of ascension came up again and I was asked,

"Do you believe that ascension is possible?"

My response was, "With God anything is possible."

At that point I realized I had been lying awake in bed all night, and I was still awake. The hour was early and the light was beginning to slowly shine through the window. The radio had been on since I'd crawled into bed at around eleven o'clock the night before, but for some reason I could not hear it. Instantly I seemed to be in another location altogether. I looked around to see that I was standing in an outdoor courtyard. There were trees which surrounded a statue of a saint I did not know, and while the wind blew the trees from side to side, I could feel the wind on my face too, as if I were physically standing there. I could see everything in great detail.

Prior to the experience, I had not believed that something that extraordinary could be possible. I knew that I was just in my room—but then I wondered again about how it was that I could see and feel the new location I was witnessing, and that it seemed to be right before me. The experience transpired for several more minutes, and then I noticed that because it was dark, the location was perhaps on the other side of the world in a different time zone where it was still night.

In the blink of an eye I was back in my room. It was once again early morning; the sun was still shining and coming through the window. Again I entered into a conversation with whom I believed to be the archangel Gabriel. We continue having a great discussion that included the topic of transcendence, and I was inquiring into how it was that any of this experience was possible when I suddenly remembered that everything is possible with God. I began to understand that the ability to experience the essential nature of the moment all became possible with God's grace.

The conversation went on for several more hours while Gabriel helped me to see that the experience and our meeting was truly associated with divine power. I looked around the room and began to see symbols and letters covering the entire visible area of the walls, from floor to ceiling and all across the ceiling. I came to the quick conclusion that it was angelic script, and although I could not read it, I thought that perhaps it was indicating that our meeting was of great importance to those who could see it. For me, it stood as a reminder of the journey I understood myself to be on, and the journey which we had just taken together. I was assured that it was angelic script and that there was a reason for it being there.

"Then he dreamed, and behold, a ladder was set
up on the earth, and its top reached to heaven;
and there the angels of God were ascending
and descending on it!" (GENESIS 28:12).

Seeing in The Dark

I had become even more proficient in nearly everything I was completely focused upon, so I began to devise several tests that could allow for better observations of each moment. When these supernatural occurrences first began, I would practice using my memorization skills daily. I have always (thankfully) had a great memory, and when I applied my mind's eye to each moment, I found that not only was my memory working well, but I had seemed to acquire an additional attribute regarding sight.

Now I see

The first of the tests I put together was one of a simple nature. I would constantly practice committing to memory where each item was located within any given space in my home. Then I would turn out the lights and continue going about my normal actions and functions as if nothing had changed. I found that I was able to recall where each item was located simply by thinking of it. As I walked into my bathroom and closed the door, I would ensure the lights were off, walk over to the shower, and turn on the water. I would then undress normally and prepare for entering the shower. I would reach for and grab a towel just by the edges of the seem, just where I thought I would grab hold of it from and place it on the floor where I later anticipated exiting, I'd reach for and then grab the edge of the shower curtain precisely where I thought I would be, and then step in. I could see every place in great detail just as I reached for it in the dark. I sensed everything and I paid close attention to the differences within each moment as the sound of water landed on the bottom of the tub. I would next reach for the shampoo and it too would be exactly where I thought it to be, next I would reach for the soap and amazingly it was exactly where I thought it would be also. What surprised me most of all was when I would drop an item, such as the soap, I could reach down to the bottom of the tub and pick it up exactly where it lay. As this search technique progressed, I realized that if I applied this same type of practice and commitment to any object I hoped to find, I could find it almost immediately regardless of location.

I came to understand that I was utilizing both sides of my brain simultaneously—I was thinking with both an analytical and creative mentality. I would reach for and acquire items in the dark with both my hands—those in different areas of proximity to one another and to myself. This technique was beginning to hold true everywhere, not just being in the shower or in my home. I could also sense when I was slightly off-balance right away and adjust myself accordingly. [What I mean by being off-balance is being slightly ahead of or slightly behind the moment I could anticipate acquiring an object or item, but I'd notice I'd be off by a fraction of a second in either direction. The readjustment I refer to requires meditation and purposeful thought techniques that helped me to sense items simply by thinking of them.] I would begin by picturing what it was I hoped to find, and once the mental image was in place, I would follow an instinctive feeling which would then become an integral part of the moment and I could then find whatever I sought simply by thought. It was as if an extension of my being had reached out spiritually to immediately find the item I was searching for and once found would become a part of my being and I would instinctively know where and how to find that which I sought simply by thought.

Seeing clearly

The second test of the moment was designed from the first and created to also work off of simple consideration of an item, object, or location. I could mentally see many of the items I was searching for in several different ways. I would first begin by meditating and aligning my chakras. Once I felt myself in complete attunement with the moment, I would focus on the item in question and gain a mental picture of it, regardless of its location. I can describe it as being able to view remotely. I had heard of remote viewing before, but I really wasn't too sure at the time how it was all possible. I empirically observed each aspect of how the moments would begin, what they produced, and how they would conclude. I found that within my heightened state of awareness, I could literally see other places in the world simply by thinking about them. Sometimes people, places, and objects would just come into a mental perception or image and I could see them or it clearly.

Other countries

The first time I realized I remotely viewed another
location, I saw a vision of it as if I were physically there.
It was a clear afternoon, and after reaching a heightened
state of awareness, instantly I was on a small watercraft
moving in the direction of a large city. The city was clearly
a foreign city, and I noticed several others on a boat with
me who appeared to be of Far Eastern descent. As I looked
toward the city skyline, I noticed tall buildings I was not
sure where we were, but I found the view fascinating. The
experience lasted for several minutes. I was surprised that
I could feel the motion of the waves as if I were personally
on the watercraft. I could hear those on the watercraft
speaking and I could see them clearly and in person. I
wondered if I could do it again and if could I control it,
and if I could control it, then how? I slowly lost focus and
the view of the city and this experience concluded.

I thought about this moment and how this remote
view was even possible and then several weeks later I had
another viewing experience. I was in my room, meditating
and experiencing a concentrated moment of energy, when
suddenly I felt an image come into focus. It was closely
comparable to someone having flipped a switch within,
and my eyes suddenly changed channels. I could see
a large stadium of sorts. Thousands and thousands of
vehicles were in a parking lot, and I could tell the event
was over because people had begun to exit the stadium
and walk towards their vehicles.

My view was from outside the stadium or arena, and
I seemed to be positioned thirty to forty feet above the
ground. In an instant, I was within one of the vehicles as it
left the stadium parking lot. I could see each intersection
we crossed in great detail. The car ride lasted for over
twenty blocks, but what surprised and astonished me the

most were the exact details of the entire experience. I was intrigued as to how it all happened in a flash-forward sequence which lasted for several minutes. My experience of each second was as if I were moving at a normal speed—but the motion of the people, the movement of the vehicles, the lights changing, the people crossing in the streets, the people exiting the stadium, the natural elements, and everything everywhere else hurriedly moved about. The moment concluded soon after it began, but I recall thinking it was perhaps someone else's memory I had somehow caught a glimpse of, someone else's emotions I was sensing; however, this amazing flash-forward sequence of all the movements within this experience was intriguing.

I had been within one of the vehicles that had left the stadium and we moved along the road in an incredibly fast way, yet each detail I recalled was brilliant and distinct and memorable. I was even sensing the sounds and scents associated at each location we passed. I began to understand and see several of the differences in the remote viewing occurrences. As the views began to increase in frequency, I began to note similarities between the experiences—how they were becoming more telling and how each of them began and how each of them concluded.

Particles of energy

I started to focus more on the movement of particles—a specific phenomena that would appear just moments before each vision, and my curiosity drove me to better understand their workings and overall function within each of the visions. I found that while concentrating diligently in meditation, tiny particles of energy began to move across my line of sight. I could tell these particles were coming from the energy resonating from everything within the moment, everything that was visibly before me. Each vision's beginning would start with many of these tiny, lightly covered particles of energy falling like snowflakes. They would move faster and faster in uniformed directions, generally from top to bottom and separated by what seemed to be millimeters. I noted that the energy particles (tiny light-colored atoms) sped up in such a way that each of them joined to form a straight line across my line of sight. The line of tiny particles would merge and then rotate in a counterclockwise direction for a few cycles; then an image would instantly appear.

Connections

I had gone in search of connections we have to each moment and, in the process, I seemed to find a glorious symmetrical connection to everything. I was still utilizing the same empirical observation techniques while experiencing this psychic phenomenon. These experiences continued to answer more questions and teach great lessons, though I found that still wasn't enough. I needed to know how and why this was happening and what this observation would lead to.

Finding the balance

I focused once again on meditation in hopes of better grasping the physical beauty of my interactions with these tiny energy particles. That night I centered my research on searching for the highest order of truth, and I went about my usual routine for observation. I focused on my breath, meditated on my surroundings, and let all else escape my attention; I then centered my thoughts on my immediate area. I suddenly felt as if I were not alone, although I was physically alone and had been all evening. I noticed a puzzling sensation coming from within; I thought that perhaps I was experiencing some form of desire for another meeting, but the feeling did, indeed, lead to another encounter with a supernatural being. The meeting began with a mental conversation and inquiry into my past misdeeds and unfortunate occurrences apparent within my life. At the time I thought I had not always made the right decisions, and sometimes I would experience the consequences of choosing the wrong ones. The narrowest path is not always easily understood, and when truth becomes difficult to comprehend, it becomes an even greater challenge to understand the correct path.

I believed myself to be in the presence of the archangel Gabriel once again. The conversation centered on balance. I had come to understand how delicate a balance all of our lives have. Because of all which had recently come to light, I realized that my life, in particular, could be comparable to a scale with one precisely set measuring point on each side. When my emotions or thoughts (either positive or negative) were applied to either side, they would tip the scale. I was also beginning to truly understand the importance and power of penitence. I still had many negative emotions and thoughts that led to my inability to obtain a perfect state of bliss. I had gotten close, but I did not quite have the ability to implement the insight. I'd had hopes of obtaining it. Then I was told that because of the life that I was living that I was the very best one and the very worst one at the same time. I didn't want to understand that truth, but I needed to. I was then told about the observations many angels were making of my life—that I was not living the one life I should. After I had heard that difficult perspective, it was then pointed out that I was living two incomplete lives as opposed to one complete one. Next, it was as if the door to humility had opened—not only did I recognize my misdeeds; I spoke them aloud, one by one, and I seemed to leave an inventory of them in exchange for gratefulness. I mentally and verbally repented for all my sin and asked God for forgiveness.[49] I hoped and prayed to live better and to do well, to be more selfless, to give more for others without expectation, and to change for the better. It was at that point I truly began to see in the dark. I thought of something I once read: "For once I was blind, but now I can see," and that, too, seemed to take on a whole new meaning to me. Our conversation had led into an appreciative acknowledgement of the wonderful truth that we can exchange our misdeeds for gratefulness. All we have to do is ask God for forgiveness.

As the spiritual meeting continued, and noting the lights were still off, I saw there appeared to be many flat and distorted people that were just on the outskirts of my peripheral vision. I had seen them before when concentrated moments of energy would allow for it, or sometimes when I'd achieved a higher state of awareness. The clarity and detail was astonishing now, and I could see the distortion of the flat individuals was caused by their different movements. Their physical attributes were similar to what we perceive as normal. I wasn't quite sure at the time the relevance or importance of such an encounter but I knew they were probably of great importance within the moment so I made note of them and continued forward.

The paths of truth and deceit

As I've mentioned before, our emotions come in two different ways: one affects our negative side of balance—when tipped it can cause specious emotions and scattered thoughts—and the second affects our positive side of balance—affecting our positive emotions and thoughts. I

---

49   Sin: An act, thought, or way of behaving that goes against the law or teachings of a religion

understand them to be a path of truth and a path of deceit. The path of truth and belief of the truth keeps one on a straight and narrow path. To acknowledge, understand, and accept truth allows us to interpret all that we perceive in this world and beyond.

It's when we discover an untruthful path that it becomes far more critical to resolve our misunderstandings of life. One experiencing such a negative path tends to question the truth that one has already known as truth. Misinterpreting the truth directly misleads and misguides one's thoughts and emotions. Fears, doubts, and disbeliefs can then be considered for a truth other than actual truth. This tends to flood one's perceptions with multiple choices, faster and faster, along with alternate scenarios offered again and again, over time continuing to mislead one who entertains such emotions or thoughts in place of truth. When we allow ourselves to be swayed toward such a path and doubt the truth, we become susceptible to the offerings of different paths other than the truth and we can (mistakenly) choose incorrectly.

When one allows for such an alternate truth, however brief a fable, one allows oneself to be misled. Paranoia becomes likely at this time. Misunderstanding leads to doubt, doubt leads to fear, fear leads to panic, and paranoia could set in; while consideration of each specious thought, or emotion, or fable, which would then be considered as a truth, continues. When we lose control over the ability to determine, decide, and conclude upon the truth in a positive direction, our emotions and thoughts can be assaulted, which in turn can bring forth such specious thoughts and emotions.

"But also for this very reason, giving all diligence,
add to your faith virtue, to virtue knowledge, to

*knowledge self-control, to self-control perseverance, to
perseverance godliness, to godliness brotherly kindness,
and to brotherly kindness love, For if these things are
yours and abound, you will be neither barren nor
unfruitful in the knowledge of our Lord Jesus Christ.
For he who lacks these things is shortsighted, even to
blindness, and has forgotten that he was cleansed from
his old sins. Therefore, brethren, be even more diligent
to make your call and election sure, for if you do these
things you will never stumble;"* (2 PETER 1:5-10).

Reaching Zen

Once I had repented my sin and asked God for forgiveness
and the gratefulness ensued, my perspective of everything
had once again changed. I could see now I was humble, I
then realized I had come to reach what one may be referred
to as a state of Zen. I was completely in tune spiritually with
all that surrounded me. I felt here, there, and everywhere
all at once. For the first time, I knew that I had attained
spiritual truth and enlightenment, in every sense of the
word. Not only was that state joyful and wondrous, but it
also brought forth, for the first time, an inner spiritual
light that shone from within. It was bright and radiating a
regal color I'd not seen before from anything.

While the inner light was shining, the conversation I
had been having reached another pinnacle when I heard
a voice say,

"You should see how you look from up here."

I was in a perfect state of emotion. I felt cleansed of
every negative aspect within my life. I was completely in
awe of the glow that seemed to emanate from within and
shine outward. The lights were still off and yet I could
see the flat and distorted people who were just on the

outskirts of my line of sight, had now begun to gather by the masses directly before me. I mentioned them before— about how astonishing their movements were and that they communicated with me in a telepathic way. What amazed me most of all was the fact that I was experiencing it from the perspective of a complete and rational person.

I looked around and I was neither here nor there; I was in the beyond yonder. I began to think of Yahweh again, and then I was asked by many of these flat and distorted beings if I knew Yahweh. Suddenly numerous questions were being asked of me. I mentally thought of responses to several of them right away when I once again began to observe the inner light resonating from within; it was shining out like a beacon to all those who were around me. Then the celestial being I was in conversation with told me that the light could be seen over four hundred and fifty miles away, and that beings were coming from all around to see the luminescent glowing light. I carefully observed the color once more; it was light blue, and white, peaceful, and brilliant. I was then told that I could continue to answer all their questions if I chose to; it was entirely up to me. My magnificent journey had led me there—into such an awakening of existence and spiritual awareness.

Discovering the truth

I focused on my experience for some time after that meeting concluded, especially on understanding the inner-workings of how enlightenment had occurred, and what others must have felt on experiencing attainment of something similar.

Although I was not experiencing any form of doubt or fear, I could clearly see that the uncertainties I once experienced within my past had once brought forth such scattered thoughts and negative emotions that hindered and possibly detoured me from having reached this state sooner. It was soon after my spiritual perspective grew, and I rose above all that I once thought to be limiting, that I attained enlightenment. The entire moment had been completely revealed within this fascinating encounter as a core truth.

What was important for me to understand was that everyone's emotions and thoughts carry as much weight as any verbal conversation does. The overall moral of that experience, I believe, is this: When you boldly discover the truth of your reality, you are enabled to continue to bring forth all you can imagine. If you can believe it, you can achieve it.

Changes became evident in everything I saw, in everything I felt, and in everything I did. I had awakened to such a beautiful day. It was midmorning; the sun had already risen, the sky was clear, and trees were swaying as the wind gently blew. I stepped into the kitchen and gazed out of the window and I heard a butterfly flap its wings. I thought, *How appropriate—an observation of the perfect and beautiful butterfly that goes through a metamorphosis in this amazing world.* I could relate to it: I felt as I had just gone through a metamorphosis myself. For the first time, I could instantly tell where everything was geographically within each moment. My senses felt as if they were at their maximum settings. I could feel the reality of my surroundings. The sun even gleamed differently than before, it shone brighter and it was here in this enlightened perspective that I felt the truth of the sprit and the importance of attaining enlightenment.

The how and the why

I found there is very little collective information on experiences comparable to mine. The Holy Bible speaks of similar experiences, and I found several stories of people who shared comparable moments, but I found it difficult to find exact details. So I began searching more intensely for anyone who could explain things in greater detail— what the spiritual and heavenly meetings were about, the essential steps that led up to the transpiration of the occurrences, and what the significance of the experiences was for.

I found many who quickly dismissed the topics as occult phenomena: possibly due to a lack of understanding these moments and how/why they form. I also found psychologists and philosophers—people who were extremely close to ascertaining the truthful insight necessary for such observations—for some reason hadn't completed their studies. Perhaps they too were stopped because of lack of understanding how/why. Though I was particularly interested in their interpretations of the conscious and the subconscious, and how we as people tend to utilize the religion we are born into and then tend to progress individually in a transcendental way. [50,51,52] I wondered how and why our conscious and subconscious worked toward our understanding of faith, spirituality and even religion and what caused us to only be able to get so far, and then begin our search for a greater understanding. I pondered the question, *what is the truth that we as people needed to grasp to rise above it all.*

A new perspective

I thought more about my perceptions, now enlightened, and how I used to perceive many things in regards to the

---

50   Conscious: The part of the mind that is capable of thinking, choosing, or perceiving
51   Subconscious: Mental activity not directly perceived by the consciousness
52   Transcendental: Relating to mystical or supernatural experience and therefore beyond the material world

world. I knew that water is wet and that the sky is blue, but it's when I awoke to enlightenment that everything I thought I knew required another look. Often that second look would allow for another perspective altogether. Take a song, for example, now listened to with a greater understanding—even a song would have a different meaning, or how a glimpse into a spiritual realm that's within each of our lives, this perspective allowing us all to grasp just how wonderful our spirit truly is. Thoughts like those would have seemed far-fetched before spiritually awakening. It was only now that my eyes are wide open and my spirit enlightened that my insights and understandings had come to know a deeper level of discernment. I know now those moments happened through discipline, persistence, concentration, and perseverance. I would come to fully understand what it meant to be in the world but not of it.

> *"And do not be conformed to this world, but be transformed by the renewing of your mind, that you may prove what is that good and acceptable and perfect will of God." (ROMANS 12:2)*

Something for everyone

Thinking again of the remote viewings I'd previously experienced, I focused once more on how the entire experience would happen, and I realized they would (almost magically) appear right before my eyes. I instinctively knew there was an explanation to all of this and I had hoped to grasp this truth. I had already been privy to certain pieces of the complex puzzle we know as life, and I believe this to be one of the motivating factors that kept me going at this point, simply because I knew that there was something I'd missed that allowed for the remote viewings to happen. I was completely unprepared for what would happen next.

Love in a Sunset

The meditation techniques that I learned and practiced now, more than ever, were beginning to yield even more phenomenal results. I would begin almost every one of my incredible experiences in a similar form. I was now driven, and I felt the truth ever so close.

- I would first start by fasting for several days.
- I then prepared my mind for expectations of the supernatural. (The fact that I did not know what to expect helped me to be mindful of each moment. It also helped add to my remembrance of each moment as it arrived.)
- I utilized the same meditation and systematic procedures that I had come to learn. (I would ensure I was alone, sitting down or in the lotus position, wearing comfortable clothing made of natural fabrics, focusing on the cycle of my breath, and clearing my thoughts and emotions until I reached a state of peace and tranquility.)

- I would open myself up to the limitless possibilities of the spiritual knowledge yet to be discovered.
- It was only at that point that I knew I could and would move forward fearlessly.

I seemed to encounter otherworldly phenomena often, and what was initially confusing for me was deciphering all that I was learning. I found that sometimes it could take long periods of contemplation just to analyze each moment—moments such as out-of-body experiences or astral projections, moments of translucent imaging of unknown people and places or events, and moments of remote views—all of the experiences needed resolution and understanding to better know what the driving sensation was that first ignited within me years earlier.

Translucent images

I then began to make observations of translucent images—a type of phenomenon that I understand has been observed and documented for thousands of years. Ancient civilizations such as that of the Mayas, Ancient Persians, Egyptians, early Native Americans, and even Tibetans all have accounts of spiritual people within their society that have experienced this form of translucent image perception I've encountered.

I noted immediately that the images would appear similar to a mental image of something that is not present, or is not considered real—an image from the direct results of our imaginations. The intriguing aspect of the images, though, is how directly they related to my emotions and thoughts. When the translucent images first began, I experienced them as subconscious insights into my existing reality. I noticed the insights had many facets and layers that, once properly observed and interpreted, would give way to great spiritual knowledge and truth.

While in a heightened state of awareness, I have observed that the conscious and the subconscious both seem to merge in a way that allows intricate combinations of events to transpire. I considered events of the past and how some seers were able to interpret what they saw. There have been prophets who could foretell the future course of events through translucent images and visions such as these. There have also been many psychics whose sensitive sight allowed similar experiences to reveal wondrous events in history. What I found were those translucent images had become somewhat controllable and were beginning to reveal insights into people, places, and things.

When these translucent images first began I had already observed many remote views, and I noted right away that the translucent images were different in appearance and form than the remote views. The remote viewings were of people, places, and things, but visually it appeared as if I were directly at the location I was seeing; while these new and other translucent images would appear as an image overlay on my true vision and perception of reality. I knew that both the image overlays and the remote viewings happened in direct correlation to the significance of my emotions and thoughts, so I moved forward with that key of knowledge at the forefront of my studies.

The images had started when my emotions or thoughts centered on something significant within my life. I was able to deduce that by focusing and giving earnest consideration to that (and while in a heightened state of awareness), the translucent images would reveal many insights into truth in my life. I was a bit mesmerized because I was able to see otherworldly places and images of people who were of importance to me within my life. Differentiating between this world and other people was not difficult. My difficulty came from learning to understand that which *is* otherworldly and learning for what reason I was encountering those knowledgeable meetings and lessons.

Visions and images

I have always considered myself a devout man, and it was during that part of my journey that I really discovered the distinctions within balance—a spiritual balance that became visible through encounters with both angels and demons. For those of you in the world who have the foolish audacity to believe that there is no such thing, perhaps this manuscript will assist in opening your eyes. Angles and demons began revealing themselves during otherworldly encounters, visions, and images. The otherworldly places I was shown were of different realms, and I was having spiritual encounters during and before the visions occurrence. At times I saw myself soaring through the air with white clouds and at other times I saw structured walls made of different stone with different forms and proportions, sometimes they would extend upward as far as I could see without a visible ceiling. Other times depending on my emotional conviction, I could periodically see pleasant and picturesque landscapes reminiscent of something biblical and yet otherworldly. The visions would last for as long as I stayed earnestly focused.

The visions and image perceptions continued nightly for many months, and although I could not yet understand their importance or significance, I instinctively knew to pay careful attention, and that I was supposed to continue. It was during that period of observations that I began to witness many forms of spiritual image, visions and celestial encounters.

Early on in my journeys I felt as if I were physically flying over mountains, clouds, beautiful landscapes, and many other intriguing locations. I often saw enormous clouds very near and felt a unique sensation as I "flew." The images and visions would appear diffusely in front of me and then peel away to reveal other wondrous sites directly behind them.

One experience that stands out in my memory was of a rugged and beautiful mountainous terrain—as unique a world as I had ever seen. Beautiful sky's and rugged mountains and as I approached this seemingly remote location, I could see what first appeared to be shallow holes on the side of a mountain cliff. I was being flown and as I got closer, I could then see that the holes were large and extremely rocky nests, at least ten feet in diameter. There were hundreds or perhaps even thousands of them, spread out about thirty or more feet apart, along the side of the mountain. We flew up the side of this wondrous mountain and then over the edge of its peeks and onto the plateau top of the mountain area, where there were many more nests. We flew following along the top of the mountain range until we came to the beginning of a great wall, which ran along the length of the mountain top and toward another structure altogether. It was over twenty feet tall and thirty feet wide. We followed the wall toward a large structure that resembled an ancient building. When I reached this place I could see its structure was enormous. I thought about who and where this place is and I was told its name, and then I was told I could not repeat its name. I didn't quite understand all that was happening to me. I realized the flight lasted for hours and then, instantly, I was back where I first began—back in my room. I would later find out that I'd been at the home of giant eagles, and the eagles were teaching me how to fly. I was beginning to learn what this journey was all about and where it would ultimately lead.

Astral forms

I can remember the evening another type of translucent
image revealed itself. I was completely aware of how it
began and of its intrinsic characteristics. I would describe
it as an extension of my subconscious, but what astonished
me was that there were other individuals in the image
who were important to me (as with my ailing aunt), who
appeared as astral projections of themselves. The astral
projections differed from the translucent images but
carried the same characteristics—they both seemed to let
the background landscape come through diffusely—but
the astral projections (of sorts) seemed to communicate with
me, as if to establish future relations. The projected types
of translucent images did not only appear by themselves,
but with whoever was of significance in relation to each
thought or emotion I was having.

I now understand these astral forms were the result
of a subconscious collective that works similar to how our
thoughts and imaginations do, and they allow all of our
relationships and current actions and interactions to bring
forth our future reality. They predetermine our future
courses before, and even while, we physically enter into
the actual relationship with whomever we are destined
to interact with. I understand now that in that place of
collective subconscious we can determine who should, or
should not be in our lives, and then proceed accordingly
towards our future.

A collective subconscious

I was in a heightened state of awareness one evening when
I reached and entered the doorway to what I believe is
our collective subconscious (which I have talked about
in previous chapters). I realized I was interacting with a
woman I had just met the evening before. I had already

made several distinct observations of these types of encounters, and I noted right away her attraction to me, although we had only met the night before.

What I gathered from this encounter was that the woman's astral projection was attempting to interact with me spiritually in an affectionate manner because she hoped to enter into some type of relationship with me. I communicated with her in a telepathic way and made it clearly evident that I was not ready to get into a relationship with her. I felt perhaps I may not have been forthright when meeting with her earlier that night and I felt that I had much work to do on myself, my life, and my research. Although our meeting earlier that night, and even our conversation on the phone, would have suggested otherwise, we never spoke again. I found that happened because of our truthful spiritual interactions within our collective subconscious, a place where we spiritually interact with one another daily/nightly.

I experienced similar encounters like this one often, and I noticed I would interact periodically with those in my life whom I deemed important or those who were in my heart emotionally. I had read certain psychologists' writings referring to the existence of the collective subconscious, but to finally have a better visual understanding of it was beginning to fascinate me. I studied and observed more occurrences of the interaction, and when I entered the doorway/vestibule of the collective subconscious, I knew then that we interacted with each other outside of reality. We show our true selves and our true emotions for one another there, and then come to our conclusions in regards to our present and future relationships. We determine the course of all our relationships with one another, make truthful decisions, and move towards our futures in this spiritual place.

Becoming visible

It was several weeks after this observation when I had a different kind of experience. I felt and saw, for the first time, what I thought to be a demon. On that particular evening my emotions were many and my thoughts were scattered. I had been walking a fine line on a narrow path, and I seemed to step into unfamiliar territory. During the observational evening, I noted there was something else present in the room, and I determined the something to be a demon or an incubus.[53] I had been in search of the essence of truth for many nights. I had been studying and practicing many different ways to reach this informative place where absolute truth resides. I recall I had a candle lit, the hour was late, and I felt uncertainty and fear. I saw a shadow change form from the shadow of my dresser into the figure of a dark demon, and before I knew it, I felt as if I were in a battle. The battle was fought within my mind over each fearful thought and misguided illusion. The demon had struggled and come to an end the moment I began to pray and humbly ask God for help. As the confidence within me began to be restored and my perspective changed from one of fear to one of courage, I heard a lion-like roar come from across the room, and then it dissipated as it reached me where I sat. I felt instantly calm, as if I had secured victory over the unwarranted encounter. I realized I had become visible to those of certain distasteful otherworldly realms.

A twelve-hour insight

---

53   Something that causes somebody much worry or anxiety, especially a nightmare or obsession

By that point of my journey, I was beginning to see events approximately twelve hours into the future. These insights would occur periodically and in a bright flash sequence, like someone feeding me an image of something random. When it happened I would generally stop each session and go in a different direction of thought, simply trying to make sense of it all. I found it confusing to grasp something truthful yet something without any reference to any thing or any time. I found it intriguing to feel the occurrence as it happened and it took several weeks before I could actually notice the twelve-hour insight transpiring, but after I passed the learning and transitional phase, I began to interpret what I had seen twelve hours previously, at the moment of its arrival. Determining the exact moment, however, and trying to decipher what it was that I was experiencing at the time of inception, was proving to be the most difficult aspect of the experience. The predictive moments would vary depending on my observational abilities per session, and when they occurred, the experience was similar to déjà vu. I would simply see the moment and what I had experienced approximately twelve hours earlier would then make sense to me. I thought it was a pretty interesting observation and so I noted its occurrence and continued.

Transcendence

It was while I was experiencing these future courses of somewhat predictable events that I became more intrigued with quantum physics. I hoped I could find a way to accurately describe this phenomenon. I'd noted there were certain particles traveling through space and time in an undetectable way, and the way they moved intrigued me. I found that neutrinos mysteriously travel (mostly) undetected from our stratosphere to reach earth. The truth of the particles' movement inspired me, and I needed to know how they moved, so I began researching the principal of particle physics and discovered that space and time were truly navigational. Although I did not have the specifics of this truth yet, simply knowing the truth allowed for one of my greatest observations—transcendence.[54]

As I thought back to the visions and translucent image perceptions of the people, places, and things I'd seen, I knew that if I altered my thoughts and emotions I could change what and who I interacted with within that grand collective area. Experimenting with that idea, I switched my thoughts to focus on another friend with whom I had recently spoken. His spiritual/astral projection appeared once again, almost instantaneously, but with another figure. I knew instantly that although the spiritual/astral projections were there to interact with me, they were there primarily to interact with my emotions spiritually. I once again noticed their objective was to determine our future relations with one another. That would happen periodically throughout most of my evenings of study, and whenever I tested my theory, I was able to determine that when I communicated my desire to no longer remain in any type of relations with the projected people back in the material world, the future interactions we could possibly have had would diminish almost overnight. During that part of my journey, I found the meetings happen nightly while we sleep, and I came to understand we interact with everyone of significance in our lives this way.

What is important to understand here is that all that I have written about, prior to that moment, transpired at the same time. The insights into prescience, fate and karma, energy, remote viewings, clairvoyance and clairaudience, angels and demons, visions and out-of-body

---

54   Transcendence: To go beyond a limit or range, e.g. of thought or belief; to exist above and apart from the material world

experiences were all yielding astonishing insights into the most universally misunderstood piece of all our lives—the supernatural, and it was all happening at once.

Forms and features

I was experiencing otherworldly beings that seemed to travel and appear with the speed of thought; they could read my mind and they interacted with me in line with my emotions and thoughts, but there was something else in the moment with me that was in line with their incredibly fast movements. It was with that observation that my studies took on an entirely new perspective. I noticed the supernatural spiritual beings arriving and departing each moment. I noted that key aspects of their arrival coincided with my emotions and thoughts, and they appeared through what seemed to be a vortex (which I mentioned earlier). I noticed a vortex would appear close to my line of peripheral vision, and a celestial figure would instantly appear in the room with me.

To summarize their features again: Some of the celestial beings had the ability to change from a masculine form to a feminine form and from a feminine form to a masculine form, and each one does so periodically in its own unique way. While other beings move outwardly every time I gaze upon them. They appear to be distorted/ flat/ and changing beings. Other types of beings are in a constant state of embrace, intertwined with one another as they continuously mesh into one, rolling over one another again and again.

My experience in this grand vestibule/hallway was in an out-of-body perception, which allowed me to turn into an astral body form. It was while in that state of being that I could have remote views and visions of people, places, and things. As I thought about the forms a body could take, I began to understand how it was all becoming possible. I began noting how those encounters began, what transpired, and how they concluded.

Angels

There were numerous amounts of spiritual beings around my bed during many of the meetings; they would often first appear as a shimmer and as I looked closer, I could make out their image and then see their skin changing form right before my eyes. They would start changing within seconds of my having observed them, all differently though. One would sparkle from one point on its form, and a metamorphosis would then follow. Another would change as translucent waves rolled over their being to reveal another being altogether. Some beings would change by having what appeared to be layers of birdlike feathers rolling over one another in synchronicity until it looked like yet another being, however, it was still the same being but in another form. They all would then periodically reverse themselves as we conversed and moved about. Often I could not utter another word, other than amazing, while they changed. I simply observed their movements, characteristics, and their beauty, and when I gazed upon them more closely I could see they changed to reveal their opposite gender, I thought I'd never seen anything quite as lovely and as impressive as them in my entire life.

The distorted and flat spiritual beings that moved outwardly every time I gazed upon them would also change right before my eyes—they changed differently though, they were always in a constant state of movement yet still had the defining characteristics of a human face. Their eyes, ears, noses, and mouths constantly changed, and they were of different sexes and ethnicities. They all had characteristics similar to humans—height, weight, hair—

all helping to differentiate one from another. For some reason, their facial characteristics changed constantly from one set to another, in a movement unfamiliar to me.

I also noticed the way that most of them seem to move within the moment. They would glide or hover in a particular manner, and some also changed from an astral body into a mass of fine particles and relocated from one side of the room to the other. The beings changed positions on a path which had the curve of an arch, and upon arriving at another location within the room, they would reform from the mass of fine particles back into an astral body. I would later understand them to be archangels.

Unique movements

At times, merely feet away from where I sat, some of the supernatural beings would embrace one another and begin to become intertwined in a constant state of embrace for several moments. When each intertwined embrace would conclude, each of the spiritual beings would continue on with its existence. Periodically, they would enter into another embrace, perhaps with another supernatural being that was close by. I could not understand exactly how or why they embraced one another in such a way; I thought perhaps it was a way for them to show affection towards one another, or maybe that was simply the way they always are. I wasn't too sure about this but I found all of their movements fascinating.

Listening to music

I constantly played music and I could see that they had an interest in my genre of music, and in each of the artists playing. Inquisitive as to who it was that was being played, they asked me what's the name of this song and who the artist playing. They all really seemed to enjoy this spiritual meeting and these wondrous moments of discovery, and sometimes they were even dancing about. Many of them would periodically get up and start to dance and move to the music.

In one experience the room suddenly grew in size to a larger one—approximately three thousand square feet—with two entrances/exits which the embracing beings arrived and departed through. There were large groups of the intertwined/rolling beings in a constant state of embrace. In the center was an opened area and lining the room were booths and couches, where many of the beings would congregate. The room was slightly dark with a very distinct atmosphere.

We seemed to communicate with expressional gestures and through my thoughts. I noted the beings to be extremely inquisitive of me and a bit uneasy with our communications. It was like the meeting was unplanned and we were learning of each other's presence cautiously.

Their actions were intriguing and I learned what I could. I would hear their questions in my mind in regards to the music I was playing and in regards to my thoughts. They all seemed to be inquiring into what I was about and what I stood for, and as I mentally responded, our conversations occasionally continued.

I noticed they would dance often in turns, in groups, and intertwined with one another; and so I, too, would begin to dance. I physically sat up from where I was positioned (lying on my bed), stood up, and I began to dance in the dark with the beings and angels. The atmosphere within my room had changed. I continued to dance to the music, but I could not physically see my room.

I was in the beyond yonder, between somewhere and nowhere at the same time, between here and there, perhaps another realm. I love to dance to great music, and I would stop between songs I did not particularly care for. I would sit down and then restart when the music I cared for began to play again. It felt like the meeting had lasted for several hours when I noticed that as I sat down, these celestial beings would come in for a more up-close-and-personal look at me. I looked to the left and to the right, and many angels began to fill the areas round me. I could see each of their movements and gestures clearly.

Mystified

As the night progressed, I continued to converse with some of them. I would ask questions periodically about that spiritual meeting, and they would sometimes ask me about my music, or other observations they were making within the moment but mostly I just observed them and they observed me. As I became more comfortable with these meetings, I began to move about within the larger rooms. I was completely mindful of each being's presence and position. They were mystifying and enigmatic at the same time. I wondered if perhaps I was a bit mesmerizing to them, too.

At that point I could tell that it had become a remarkable meeting, on both sides, by the way I was now being observed. Larger groups of these supernatural beings were visiting often. It was like they had told their friends to come by and have a look at this new person they found. I could clearly see the differences in all their genders and in their appearances. Although we all had become noticeable to one another, it was an unfamiliar experience for me. The intertwined constant embraces, the meetings, and the dancing would all periodically cease and groups of angels would maneuver in closer to me, gaze at me momentarily, and then hurry by me. They acted as if they, too, realized it was an amazing meeting, or perhaps they may have been just as intrigued as I was that it was actually happening. The spiritual meetings continued like that nightly over the course of the next several months.

Exits and entrances

I had finally begun to see the moments of departure and arrival more clearly, and I noted in particular that the embracing beings seemed to leave through exits that were similar to hallways or doorways, but that I somehow transcended to the location they were from. They were the same beings that really enjoyed the music, the ones in a constant state of embrace.

The beings I had seen changing from masculine to feminine, and from feminine to masculine and who now had become more recognizable as archangels, would arrive and depart in another way altogether. They would change form from an astral body/their spiritual form by instantly bursting into a mass of fine particles of energy (which resembled a very light-colored shadow), and in a single thought would enter a vortex and miraculously leave the moment. At that time many different types of angels began to visit, and most reminded me of images and figures I had seen carved into stone in ancient Egypt. Some had heads of birds while others had brilliant wings, each different than the last. I was completely mesmerized at how that could be possible, despite my faith and spirituality. I knew that angels were said to have the ability to travel at the speed of thought, but what astonished me now was actually being able to see it happen.

As the evenings progressed and I observed more details of their travelling capabilities, I noticed one departure in particular that stood out more than the others had: I noticed the appearance of an angel for only a fraction of a second, but it seemed to be there for several minutes.

The angel was on my left, within arm's length, despite there being no room for anyone to be standing where he stood—my bed was pressed up directly against that side of the wall. It was then that I understood that the meeting was an extra-dimensional observance, but what astonished me was that I witnessed the angel leaving the moment—I saw how and where the departure occurred. In my heightened state of awareness, my view allowed for an incredible glimpse into this other spiritual world.

Another realm

There appeared to be another spiritual realm directly woven into this material world and it became visible as I looked to the left side of my bed, and the angel departed to that place from my bedside. As I observed this moment, I could tell that both places existed simultaneously and it could be reached from any place within the material world. I could clearly see the incredible transition— transcendence from point A, which was situated within my room, to point B, a location somewhere in another spiritual realm. I could also see the precise arrival at point B. The spiritual being stretched in an infinite manner as the angel returned from whence it came.

A different kind of view

While the spiritual realm altered itself into an unnoticeable mode of existence again, I was clearly able to see into it just before it closed—I could see an amazing matrix of spiritual locations, each one stacked on top of one another and perfectly symmetrical. They appeared similar to cubes, with a different view of a spiritual location within each block, and the number of blocks covered the entire area of my line of sight both vertically and horizontally. As I gazed upon the striking arrangement of complex entrance ways to an otherworldly dimension, I felt strongly that a complete comprehension of the exact design could be difficult for those without the capacity to grasp the vastness of multiple dimensions, realms, and kingdoms; or even navigation and ascension of them.

It took several months to truly comprehend the enormity of that precise moment. It was during that stage of development that I eventually came to the conclusion that all that I had been experiencing was of a divine nature and that the grandeur of the experience was just beginning. I was just learning about vortices and how they do in fact lead to other spiritual realms.

Why me?

The idea that I had become as sensitive to encounters with these beings was still somewhat perplexing. I knew, however, that I was experiencing and interpreting moments beyond the natural range of most humans. Learning how the different abilities worked within my life, which aided in extraordinary perspectives, took much practice. I recall, during that immediate discovery and acceptance of clairvoyance, a moment coupled with an exact whisper in my ear. I inquired into my past and asked how it was possible for someone such as me to have such abilities. While thinking of my interactions with the spiritual beings, I began thinking of my past relationships. I noted my self centeredness, my past occurrences with ego, and all the sins I had committed in my past. I confessed them out loud and began to pray to God, asking for forgiveness for my sins. Once again, I renounced all that was evil and gave my will to God. I humbly sought direction and understanding, and it was in that moment when I noticed the whisper become even clearer to me; at times it was conversational, but always with purpose. The interaction gave further insight into all I had been experiencing.

Supernatural tranquility

By now I knew that the path I'd taken was leading me to the real nature of perfect bliss. One particular experience and insight began in my practiced way—with several days of fasting coupled with prayer, focus, and zeal. I had been in a heightened state of awareness for numerous hours, and had given my will to God and asked for forgiveness. I felt more humility in my life than ever before.

With Gods blessing, I focused on my breathing once again. I continued to align myself, placing my hands over my chakra energy points and utilizing breathing techniques. I began to tune and align my body's energy just like an instrument. To my amazement, I could feel each chakra moving in what felt like different directions and speeds, so I placed one hand over the other and then over each chakra point on my body, paying close attention to each chakra's energy spin cycle . . . until . . . I could visibly see the celestial being I believed to be an angel of God—the same being who had spoken with me for many months.

During our subsequent conversation, I learned how rare my experiences were. The conversation had gone on for nearly an hour until the moment when I mentally hoped for peace, tranquility, and penitence. I then noticed the angel in an astral body directly near my body . . . and then something wonderful happened. I saw the angel extend an appendage/arm, and gracefully inserted it into my body, where it grabbed hold of the chakra energy point directly in the middle of my torso, my heart chakra. It was moving at a faster rate than my other chakra points, and after several seconds I could feel the chakra point slow down to spin in unison with the other energy points. I could tell that several others were out of alignment as well, and I believed the angel could also. As the process continued over the next few minutes, I began to feel what I had hoped for—tranquility. I felt perfect alignment of my mind, body, and spirit. It was at that exact moment I lost myself and found myself at the very same time. I truly felt sanctified as the awe-filled moment reached its pinnacle. I realized nirvana and began to brightly radiate a blue-white light coming from the center of my body. I once again attained complete enlightenment. [55,56] I realized I may not have been able to reach that spiritual pinnacle had it not been for the alignment of my chakras and the aid of that celestial being, that angel. I was grateful and carefully considering all that had to have happened for this meeting to occur.

Different yet the same

A spiritual meeting then ensued between myself and the angel of God and then I heard,

"James, I've never seen anything like you before." I asked the angel, "Before like in the last few years or before like ever?" The angel responded saying he was referring to, like ever. I was not sure how to respond to that. I thought surely there must be others who can spiritually see and interact with the supernatural in such a way as what I have been seeing.

My response to his first statement was, "I'm just like everyone else, right?" I had been telling myself that often because I didn't quite understand exactly what I had been

---

55   In Hinduism, Buddhism, and Jainism, the attainment of enlightenment and freeing of the spiritual self from attachment to worldly things, ending the cycle of birth and rebirth
56   The realization of spiritual or religious understanding, or, especially in Buddhism, the state attained when the cycle of reincarnation ends and human desire and suffering are transcended

learning. For me to continue moving forward, I had to try to convince myself that my experiences and insights were of a common occurrence to everyone. The conversation then changed to one of an ecumenical nature.[57] It was there that I learned that I had inherently seemed to practice all forms of spirituality simultaneously. I then said,

"It felt natural and correct to practice and combine the practices of all the different spiritualities."

I know I have talked about this before, but in the moment, I wasn't sure what it meant to fully practice all the spiritualities all at the same time. I wasn't even sure where the reference was going. I'd believed and practiced in that manner because it instinctively felt like the right way. I believe there are many paths in life and we all must find our own, but I truly believe, with all that I am, that if we try and tell life what it is supposed to be, it limits what it could possibly be. I have found this holds true not only with this ecumenical insight, but with all facets of life. I believe the message here is faith in God and that we all have the abilities within us to experience these types of supernatural occurrences when we open ourselves up to the truth of existence.

Sunset

It was with that enlightened realization that I thought to mentally invite the angel to join me to watch the sunset at a special place. I was told yes, but before I left my room, we had conversations about my health and the importance of taking better care of myself—mainly living right and making better choices in regards to each moment, and with others.

It was springtime and still slightly cool outside. I prepared for my journey and then began to drive towards

57   Ecumenical: Involving or promoting friendly relations between different religions

145

a special place within my city called Mt. Bonnell—the highest hill to overlook the city and a portion of Lake Austin. The most important aspect to the place, other than giving one the ability to see the entire city at the southeast point and the hill country to the west, is that it allows one to see the incredible sunsets that take place there.

The entrance of the park is a stairway of one hundred and forty steps which led up the rugged hilltop. I thought about how appropriate that was, because I felt as if I'd just climbed another mountain of sorts; to culminate with such a physical climb was a befitting conclusion to the affair. Although the climb was not very steep and concluded within several minutes, it seemed to take my breath away. When I reached the top, I noticed dozens of others there who had had a similar desire to see the sun set—romantic couples, tourists with cameras, families, and kids—all situated around a great wooden pergola that overlooked the river. I looked nearby for several minutes before I found a table with no one around it, and I sat down on its cement tabletop. I gazed outward toward the direction of the hills, noting that I had several minutes before the sun set. I thought, *Are you there?* Naturally, I was thinking outwardly to determine if I was in the presence of the angel, and once again I heard its whisper and knew that I was truly in its presence. We began to have a conversation, and I began to think of Yahweh again—about how beautiful a creator God is and how blessed I truly felt. I snapped a few photographs of not only the beauty and appeal of the sunset, but of what I believed to be something otherworldly. I was awe inspired with each moment. I thought of how surreal a moment could possibly be when a couple of kids chased each other up to the table. They were followed by two women, both of whom came close and observed me (as protective mothers often do around strangers). Just as they came within several feet of me, I heard one say to the other in a very low voice,

"There's something that's around that guy."

Although the tone was extremely low, I distinctively knew of whom she spoke—it was the angel who was sharing the sunset with me.

As the sun set, I could clearly see how sacrosanct my day with the celestial being had become. It gave my life a perspective I had not recognized before; it helped open my eyes to the barrier of my acceptance of the truth of my abilities. I stayed at Mt. Bonnell for another half an hour, still in a mental conversation, and left as the nighttime came.

In spite of the experience, and the others before it, I was bothered that my mind seemed to sometimes revert back to its old way of thinking. I found I could sometimes take two steps back if I lost my focus on the significance of the entire experience. I knew that although the state of bliss came with incredible clarity in each moment, I still needed to learn exactly what it was I had achieved. I knew that if I were to continue with the same vocabulary, the same mindset, and actions, then perhaps I would never come to fully understand these frequent experiences and what I was truly becoming a part of.

Better expression

I prayed to God, asking for the ability to speak and communicate with greater depth. I believe I have always had the ability to speak well, but I would often not pay close attention to how I came across to others. God answered my prayer; my part was simply acknowledging the existence of the depth available and applying it to my life. I did that by incorporating several different perspectives and understandings, and one important belief.

"Rejoice always, pray without ceasing, in everything give thanks; for this is the will of God in Christ Jesus for you" (THESSALONIANS 5:16-18).

As I made it home I was approached by many celestial beings that evening and I was asked many questions about what I had seen and experienced. I truly felt blessed by the Creator himself. Many of the supernatural beings around me were hoping to catch a glimpse of what it was that I believed I had photographed earlier that afternoon with my camera phone. I was asked if I knew the way to heaven and if I knew God. I answered,

"Yes, I know God and he is a friend of mine."

The conversations continued into the night. I was asked different kinds of questions—different in nature and posed differently; they were more inquisitive as opposed to definitive. It was as if I was being tested by the celestial beings, or perhaps I was truly being asked by others who seemed to be lost, or perhaps both. I noted the differences between the ways they asked me and then made the decision to relax and unwind from my amazing, insightful encounter.

I had been privy to supernatural and celestial intrigues, astral projections, and supernatural spiritual beings; I had been in the presence of divine beauty and appeal; I had come to learn many spiritual truths. I hold every lesson in high regard, for without them—each breath and each step—I would not have arrived at that point along my path, *all thanks to God. Thank-you, God and thank-you, Jesus.*

"But by the grace of God I am what I am, and his grace toward me was not in vain; but I labored more abundantly than they all, yet not I, but the grace of God which was with me." (1 CORINTHIANS 15:10)

Devotion and Dedication

I stood at the base of a ten-thousand-foot mountain, noticing how massive it was. I could see how incredibly long the mountain's side was, and if I stared straight up its almost vertical face, I could just about see its peak. Just then, a large portion of the peak broke off and began to fall directly overhead . . . I first thought to run away as fast as possible . . . I looked up again . . . the mountain peak was heading straight for me . . . I began to pray to God . . . I closed my eyes and I put all my trust in God. I heard a loud crash and I opened my eyes to see the mountain peak fall at my side and then I thought to myself, *The power of prayer can really move mountains.* I begin the next part of my journey with that epiphany in mind.

Vectors

I would lie in bed nightly thinking about how it might be possible to travel through space and time and all that would be required (in time and space) in order to do so. With my fingertips all touching their opposites, I created the shape of a sphere with my hands. Then I thought about vectoring a location with x, y, and z axes as I rotated my wrists in circular movements. I thought about how I might find any location in space and time with the proper vectoring. I hoped to figure out the fundamental principles of how the supernatural beings were continuously arriving and departing. I understood that comprehension was more than unlikely; however, I had a strong inclination that I was on the right track.

As one particular evening began, I prepared my internal observational skills (that by that point had reached new levels). I reached a concentrated moment of energy and entered into a heightened state of awareness, just as I had done so many times before. I began to anticipate where I thought the vortices would appear. I focused on my previous observation of the openings functioning in unison with my thoughts and emotions. While the beings moved at blurring speeds on my left or on my right around me, their motion initially gave no indication of their points of entry; however, there did appear to be a quick and instant trail that was recognizable out of the periphery of my sight. I felt the truth ever so close. Although these beings were becoming more and more noticeable, I could still generally depict their fast-moving blurs. I continued to focus on thought and emotion and prepared myself for better understanding this truth. I practiced observing this occurrence for hours before needing some time to analyze the facts.

I moved from my bedroom to the living room, where I turned on the television set to relax and reflect. To my amazement, I also noticed the fast-moving blurs around other individuals on the television screen. The angels' movements also appeared to have the ability to move through the screen, through that precise point in space and time, to where I was and vice versa. Initially, I thought that perhaps I must be mistaken, because it could very well be impossible for something like that to be true. I have a pretty good understanding of physics, and I had never heard of that from anyone, ever. I paid careful attention to that observation and noted its similarities to something else rather extraordinary and my studies went in an entirely different direction at this point.

Black holes & wormholes

That observation led me to study black holes and wormholes—how they operate and what their defining characteristics are. I studied their overall significance within our universe and noticed their many similarities to other larger vortices like tornados, hurricanes, ocean waves, and every other type of similar vortex. I noticed how each vortex's energy signature, resembled a single droplet of water as it lands onto a larger body of water, its energy ripples moving outward. I began to understand that every tiny vortex I saw was somehow universally connected to another spiritual realm. I noted that I'd seen an angel transcend into another spiritual realm in the same way an object enters into a wormhole or a black hole (at least, that is what we understand so far). I noticed the matter that enters each vortex would stretch itself in an infinite manner and appeared to be smeared through space and time from point A to point B.

I looked a bit more carefully to understand what process would allow for a comparison of my theory, and my thoughts led me to investigate the way a camera operates. I could see that pieces of equipment inside a camera work together to encapsulate each moment, and they impose the image of all that the lens views onto film or tape. The images can then be developed and viewed any time thereafter. They have the same type of ability as a black hole—a moment/image can be encapsulated and viewed later. The lesson here is not on the process that takes place but on what happens during this process. I noted the camera's method of capturing the light—it slows down as it passes through the lens. In this same way, I could tell that the transcendent moments I witnessed were actually occurring at a slower pace than the moments beforehand, the slowed-down process was partially what allowed me to observe its occurrence while it instantly happened.

The event horizon

Night after night I lay in bed pondering, trying to understand this process and searching for the connection that would allow for this truth to become understandable with everything. Night after night I went over the fundamental details of every second of perception I had on entering that grand hallway or doorway to our collective subconscious. I realized that whenever I reached a heightened state of awareness and felt a concentrated moment of energy, many tiny particles of energy moved from top to bottom of my line of sight. I felt as if I were looking directly into a vortex, it was similar to the circular pupil of my own eye (which was reminiscent of a tiny black hole), and the tiny particles of energy would all increase in movement, now moving hurriedly from top to bottom. They would keep increasing in speed, moving faster and faster until they all formed a single small line of energy particles, which would then begin to swirl several times in a counterclockwise direction. This process fit with what I had learned of the event horizon.[58]

It was at that point I began to study the out-of-body experience and its role more closely. I had already encountered and noted three different types of out-of-body experiences: personal, relative, and transitional, and I felt that perhaps there was a connection between them and remote viewing. I came to the realization/conclusion that all remote views were indeed possible while experiencing an out-of-body perspective, in particular while in a transitional out-of-body state. What I noted next was that while in an earnest and considerate perspective, and while observing another point in space and time, one would remain lucid. The ability to do that allowed for remote views and spiritual insights into anything and everything everywhere.

Despite understanding that, I still didn't have the master key; I still hadn't found what made it all possible. Night after night I studied and searched for the missing truth to (what I was coming to understand as) transcendence.

A celestial transit system

I began to grasp the profundity of the thought that we are connected to everything, everywhere, and it was then that I realized that these celestial beings were arriving at and departing my locations because they were navigating vortices like a type of celestial transit system that allowed their spiritual realm to connect with our material world.

These symmetrical shaped temporal nexus locations around us all has already been documented and even filmed, and are often referred to as a vortex; but it wasn't until after I studied the visual characteristics of a

58   Event horizon: The theoretical boundary surrounding a black hole, within which gravitational attraction is so great that nothing, not even radiation, can escape because the escape velocity is greater than the speed of light

vortex that this observance truly made sense. Each video documented occurrence of a vortex seems to have three or four arched shapes on one side while the other side has the same shapes; however, the other side's slightly offset those on the first side. Having observed that phenomenal occurrence of vortices many times, I realized then that the fast moving blurs were actually arrivals and departures, and that was what I had been seeing traveling at great speeds all around me (and around others). That was the insight and discovery that allowed me to finally grasp the concept of vortices and how angels seem to move to and from this material world from their spiritual realm.

What I was able to observe was that my ability to see each vortex and supernatural/celestial being directly coincided with my emotions and my thoughts. What was completely amazing to me was that I noticed as I observed one of the vortices frontal view and entrance, I could then notice the classic vortex's circular spiral shape. I did, in fact, connect months earlier with one of the vortices in the center of my forehead. At that point I was able to determine that while in a heightened state of awareness and while completely focused on what I was hoping to ascertain a perspective of, I could enter an out-of-body transitional perspective through meditation . . . which would in turn allow for remote views . . . which would then come in view by instantly traveling through one of those vortices . . . if only for an instant . . . as if I were directly seeing each place in person.

I found it fascinating to have a direct understanding of remote views. Once that information and insight completely registered, I began to search for the celestial transit system which I believed was contributing for the remote views and every other intriguing aspect of the vortices. Fascinating as all that was in terms of discovery,

I needed to know more—why and what function a system such as that served, and where it would lead to.

I began this portion of discovery with some of those initial insights into that observation. I had wondered how it was possible to be the only one in any given moment, anywhere, and feel exactly when another person enters and lays eyes upon you. I wondered how photographs (of any place and time) could seem to come alive. I wondered how and why our emotions and thoughts were met directly by supernatural beings through this celestial and incredible transit system.

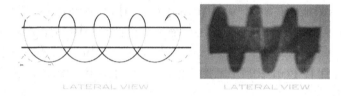

LATERAL VIEW　　　　　　　LATERAL VIEW

The missing piece

I had been experiencing that type of insight for several evenings when I finally noticed the missing piece of the puzzle—the key to how it all connected. Each moment within every place in existence carries the symmetrical signature of vortices, and each signature is of an evenly separated sphere-shaped vortex. They are extremely tiny, brilliant and separated by several inches in every direction. That understanding helped me to grasp the moment I had witnessed an angel transcend from our material world back to a spiritual realm.

I had found that the energy our chakras produce causes a ripple that is recognizable anywhere, and anytime. It was with this insight that I could clearly see the energy we exert connects with each of these vortices and that is how we are able to feel someone looking at us when we are all alone.

This is how a psychic or clairvoyant can walk into any given place and time and feel/see what has once happened there. Our energy, our emotions, and our thoughts all affect, interact, travel, and resonate along and within each of those symmetrical vortices, which means that our emotions and thoughts are not only communicated to each other, but also with the supernatural and celestial beings in the spiritual realm. This is how a photograph could seem to come alive while one is in a heightened state of awareness and focused in a concentrated moment of energy. This is also how, when we feel close to a motion picture, it feels as if we're a part of the film. The video equipment records the images and unknowingly also records the vortices which we connect to as we view the film or photos. This also works with other people everywhere I found that we instantly connect to and attach to their emotions via those vortices.

The vortices are an intricate spiritual and supernatural transit system and are part of each of our lives—they are the key to our interactions with each other and with the supernatural. They allowed for remote views, and they have aided many great truths to become understood.

I bring that to attention once again because I truly believe the interactions we have with those of other realms are of great significance in all of our lives. I also believe that those who understand such an intricate aspect of life have the responsibility to acknowledge that:

-the interactions and occurrences truly exist.

-they transpire daily in all of our lives and always have.

As I mentioned before, photographs and video recordings capture the symmetrical, evenly shaped vortices.

The vortices provide a way for an empathic connection to other locations through space and time. This is how we all truly share an empathic connection to everything. This was how I noticed the supernatural beings being able to move through space and time and this is when I knew that it was in fact possible for the connection to everything to be true.

Traveling through vortices

I noted many similarities when comparing my experiences to those described in the Bardo Thodol, also known as the Tibetan Book of the Dead.[59] Like those who had acquired the knowledge before them of the book before it had been written, I too had come to understand that there are numerous spiritual realms of existence and various stages within them. I encountered many attributes within the aforementioned manuscript that were comparable to the experiences I had undergone. What was intriguing most to me was that similar experiences in the book transpired during my life and revealed truth of the after-life.

Most importantly, I found the teachings in it comparable to many other truths regarding righteousness. I came to a conclusion, when one has faith in God and lives a truly righteous life, then navigation of the afterlife and any spiritual realm is done with love and faith. Know that with God there is nothing to fear, in this world, or in the world to come.

In my next experience, I had a sort of ringing in my ears as I reached another pinnacle of an exact moment, and many tiny particles of energy seemed to flow faster and faster before my eyes when, suddenly, they formed one straight line and rolled over in a counterclockwise

59   Bardo Thodol: Written by a Tibetan monk, the Book of the Dead chronicles the experiences and religious opportunities a person encounters at various stages: while dying, at the moment of death, during the 49-day interval between death and rebirth, and at rebirth.

direction. I had obtained an out-of-body transitional perspective and had begun to enter a vortex. When I arrived at the new location I noticed tall trees, around fifty feet tall, swaying to and fro with the wind. It was nighttime, and I was standing in a clearing in some far-off country. I saw a vehicle in the driveway of a nearby a home. I was mesmerized with what I could see, hear, and feel, and thought I was having a type of clear remote view, but then I noticed a couple standing by the car. As I observed them I seemed to move closer, and as I approached, one of them noticed me. That was a bit startling and I lost focus and made my way back home. Upon instantly arriving, I could literally see myself reforming from a mass of fine energy particles back into an astral body. I was completely mesmerized with that, because it was the first time I noticed myself in particle form. I had seen many angels in astral body form burst into fine particles of energy right before me and now, as I gazed upon myself, I knew that I was completely capable of doing the same.

That night I visited several different places around the world I had moved with several accompanying angels and was told that I had just visited four different countries around the world in one night. I wasn't sure where I had gone to or even who it was that I had traveled to see but one thing I knew for sure the places I had seen were all truly beautiful parts of this wondrous world.

A direct union with divinity

It still hadn't quite hit me what I had learned. I was in the process of deciphering it all. I did note that my timing had become impeccable. What I mean by that is that I seemed to be exactly where I was supposed to be all of the time. I was starting to be able to truly appreciate the grandeur of God's timing with everything, everywhere.

My insightful abilities had reached their apex, and I could hear the forethoughts of those in my immediate area; I could remote view to almost any place when I focused intensely enough; I could see the energy signatures of almost everyone, everywhere; I had observed prescience and understood it; I had interacted with celestial beings; I found myself navigating in a similar fashion to theirs; I could detect and anticipate future courses of events; and I felt the sensations of others empathically. I believe it was partially because of those moments that I was truly able to comprehend a direct union with divinity and see its transpiration in a very special way.

My encounters with vortices are typical of what many have claimed to have encountered with near-death experiences (NDE). I came to the conclusion that the white tunnel, that has been claimed to be seen by many, is in fact one of the vortices that exist everywhere, all the time. I found that understanding because of my perspective in out-of-body transitional experiences coupled with my faith in God and the amount of time I spent in those places.

Waiting angels

I attained a transitional out-of-body perspective one evening and felt myself begin to spiritually rise upward. There was darkness all around until I noticed a blue and white glow that once again appeared to be shining out from within me. I felt at complete peace, I knew spiritual enlightenment had been reached yet again.

I physically sensed the presence of an incredible energy nearby. I looked to my left and saw what I believed to be deity for several brilliant moments. I began to converse with the being, all the while beginning to feel a type of reserved control—a sense of inner peace I'd not felt in such a distinctive way before.

As my inner peace grew in superlative measure, instantly I realized I was no longer in my room. I felt and knew I was floating in an outdoor country setting somewhere else. I could see myself illuminating the area like a beacon. I began to fly alongside this wondrous being and we moved closer to a country house I saw nearby and, in doing so, I noticed many celestial beings scattered along the side of the home in groups of two or more. I could see some of them sitting about while others seem to be restless and fighting over a something off in the distance. They fought ferociously, and I could see their wings as they rolled over one another battling. It appeared these were the beings who would administer something like a lesson or a challenge to any person who would not walk upright. That part seemed quite evident. I moved in closer for a better look at them.

I noticed their appearance was quite distinctive. I could see their facial characteristics and their bodies' defining attributes. They were not human; I understood them to be angels, but I was not sure what kind of angels they were. Each one had a very unique appearance. Their faces were slightly elongated and they had no visible hair on their heads; their eyes were sharp and piercing, and they displayed a slight slope on their foreheads. I was at complete peace and felt serene so I moved in even closer, within inches of their faces, and looked intently upon them. It seemed the closer I got, the more still they appeared. Perhaps they were not allowed to show emotion. Again I noticed I was in spiritual form, radiating light outward through an enlightened perspective. I realized these beings were more than likely the same ones that were responsible for acting upon the negative emotions and scattered thoughts of the misled . . . . or fearful.

That supernatural perception was enlightening because I could see just how the beings existed between this world and another spiritual one, and they seemed to be merely waiting for the moment to act upon one who lacked faith or who could not defend him/herself. I found this is a truth for every person within the world. This behind the scenes spiritual insight, showed how we all must live in the truth and how we are acted upon by those angels if we chose to live in a timid and fearful way.

Remote viewing

It got to the point when I could simply close my eyes, concentrate diligently, and hope to gain another perspective of anything, and a remote view would simply show up right before my eyes (not physically, of course) but mentally.

To describe another experience: When I first entered the vortex, many tiny particles of energy entered at the same time. I attempted to calculate the velocity and angles of each particle of energy as it entered into the vortex to understand what would be necessary for the quantum mechanics of my observation to truly exist. Then the event horizon flipped a few times and I began to observe many beautiful colors moving at great speeds all around me. I was moving extremely fast at an incredible speed.

I found myself in an unknown place with many tall walls and great rooms, and many supernatural beings seemed to be there too. I focused on them to get a better view, but they immediately fled when I laid eyes upon them. I knew they were the same celestial beings I had witnessed before, and at that point I realized I had seen a similar place to this one but not in such detail. The celestial beings appeared unable to stay still; they were the same flat/distorted beings in my peripheral vision I had once encountered. The same beings that I'd previously seen within my room dancing, but now their movements were more noticeable, they were running fast, in place, but moving at a slow pace away from me. It was like they were moving hurriedly but traveled away slowly. I now understood I was in the spiritual location where they initially came from. I could see the walls and dimensions of each room, which periodically seemed to reform (at thought) and reveal another room altogether, or form an extension of the room I had previously been in. The journey lasted for only a few more minutes and then I found myself back in my room contemplating the entire moment. I decided to move forward, hoping to observe all that I could and determine the intricate aspects and greater details of the experience when it was time to do so.

A sequence

At that point I noted one particular sequence of events that seemed to be universal with the celestial transit system: I would enter the vortex each time, in similar form and fashion—with a concentrated moment of energy, focus, zeal, and meditation. Upon studying the way I had been entering, I could see that the tiny particles of energy and light were moving at extremely fast speeds, and as they sped up, I could see them all bend and then enter into the vortex. The vortex tunnel I had become so familiar with was lined with many more continuous particles of light and energy inside.

Over the next several hours of trial and error, and after my first several attempts fell short, I began learning to navigate the long cylindrical tunnels. From what I could understand, each section of this celestial transit system was comprised of three main parts. The first section and last section appeared to be the same size (about twenty feet long), and the central section was three times the length of the first and last. I slowed down within the vortex, almost to the point of stopping. I was hoping to better observe its construction. I could see the entire tunnel illuminated by a complex array of perpetual energy, but I found that if I lost focus of the visibly lit path, I would find myself back on my bed. It felt as if I were learning to drive within the tunnel. If I would happen to misread a turn to the left or the right, I would fall short and have to start all over again. The tunnel would turn, swerve, bend, and curve in directions which were difficult to maneuver. It seemed the tunnel continued in length and I had no way of determining how long it actually was, it was beyond measurement, beyond our understanding of time and space. It took me many more unsuccessful attempts at navigation before realizing I must simply stay focused and not lose sight of the proper directional path—a lesson that holds true on any plane.

It was at that point on my journey that everything finally made complete sense to me. Although I had been learning to understand the intricacies of the supernatural, it all clicked within my mind at last.

- I would enter into a heightened state of awareness.
- I would then center and focus myself for observations.
- I would obtain an out-of-body perspective.
- As I reached a concentrated moment of energy, I would navigate to a place upon which I focused intensely.
- I would not necessarily have to manually navigate each vortex—dedication to thought would assist in allowing direct attainment.
- Upon arrival I could see, hear, and sense all that was transpiring at this new location.

Despite my new level of understanding this amazing phenomenon, I found myself struggling with several personal decisions in both my past and present, which was a new experience, especially when I couldn't understand why I was having the difficulty with something I thought I already knew and understood. I was experiencing moments of conviction whose source was undetermined, but I was to find out that they were a precursor of a new lesson. I had just begun learning to navigate the celestial transit system, but at the time I didn't clearly understand it could lead to many heavenly realms. I was not prepared for what was to happen next.

My second transcendence

As the lesson began, I felt my whole body periodically tremble, both internally and externally. When coupled with my thoughts, it proved to be an overwhelming experience. I continued to think of my past misdeeds, and again I would frequently break down and cry, thinking of how low I felt. I moved forward, continuing to feel low and trembling from every other thought.

After an hour of this, I broke down crying over all I thought of. I heard the radio station delivering news of the global situation of the world, and those conflicts added to my sorrows. Every emotion I felt and every thought I had added to my downcast state, and at one point I desperately hoped to help put an end to all of the world's suffering. I didn't realize that I was being convicted of past and present actions in order to lower my opinion of myself/to bring me to an understanding of my actions, and my past misdeeds. The moments of mortification and humiliation finally concluded and I begin to meditate. I entered into a higher state of awareness, and it was during that humbled concentrated moment of energy that I suddenly felt a great sensation come over me and I transcended.

At first I didn't understand what I saw or where I was, but I came to understand I had instantly transcended into a heavenly realm. I thought it might all be a dream until I noticed a grand and magical crystal palace of many rooms. There were thousands of others moving around, dancing and listening to music and really enjoying themselves. Fascinated, I realized I was in a place with many people who had gone through the same experience as me—they were all in a humbled and lowered/abased in their estimation of self and had transcended to be with God. It was one big abasing party! I was to learn a lot about abasement in the coming years....

I was taken in by this sight, never before had I seen such a place. The atmosphere was incredible, and joyous. As I observed my surroundings, I could see many gathered all around, some were talking, some were dancing, and some singing, and all of them enjoying each other's company. Then someone walked up to me and said hello, it was God. He actually asked me what I was doing there, and after we spoke for several minutes about that moment he began to show me around, leading me from section to section and room to room. Around every bend was a larger group of people, all lovingly sharing joyous moments in abasement with God. God our Father introduced me to everyone there as we walked around, and then we came across a smaller group sitting in several rows of sectional seating, ten rows deep and twenty feet across. Everyone who was sitting was being entertained by a person singing on the stage in front of them, and suddenly I had a joyful thought which caused the lights everywhere in the entire place to flash brilliantly—my emotional state seemed to directly contribute to the atmosphere. I somehow floated directly over the group and could see everyone laughing and enjoying that great moment beneath me. Music continuously played in the background, as if it were being broadcast to the whole place. We walked around for a little while longer and then I sat down with God our Father and Jesus (who was there too) and a few others to join in conversation—one unlike anything I had ever been a part of before.

We spoke of many things, and also about how this encounter had happened. God pointed out that I had been moving in the way the many supernatural being before me had moved, I had begun to move in similar fashion to them. I thought about that for a moment and was enjoying our time together but still trying to comprehend the enormity of it all. We moved from there after a few hours to a more private yet casual setting. The four of us—God our Father; Jesus, Lord and Savior; the Holy Spirit and me—continued talking about how incredible my journey had just become. I was in awe; I was miraculously meeting with God. Our conversations covered a number of topics on subjects like abasement, transcendence, and spirituality. While I was explaining to God how I found vortices, a mental image of each detail I was explaining instantly appeared before us all diffusely, like a projection on the wall. We then talked about space and time and even about forever, and what that truly meant. Then God began to explain why I had been crying before my transcendence. The screen changed to the moments of when I was in tears and experiencing many trembling sensations and humility from hours earlier. I was in awe; I was actually witnessing myself in the past and just as we looked at the exact moment of when those feelings were transpiring. I could see that that was what was giving me those peculiar sensations. I learned a little more about abasement and conformity with him in that meeting, and I would later come to find out why I was trembling and crying.

Although the experience was wonderful to be a part of, I didn't know how to stay in the presence of God. I didn't really understand the proper state of abasement, nor did I know how to keep God first in my life. As that wonderful meeting concluded, I found myself back at home once more pondering the events.

I thought about when I broke down crying, and I realized I had experienced similar emotional feelings several times before—when I was first told of being in God's grace, when tears of joy would stream at unexpected moments, when I acknowledged blessings from God—those moments showing me what it meant to be completely taken in with God. I had considered myself a faithful man all of my life, but whenever I thought again of what it meant to be a part of such a sacred journey, each realization brought forth more tears that would allow me to feel an over—whelming and peculiar sensation. I knew each holy experience was a gift from God, and then I heard a voice say,

"Many tears will come uncontrollably; you are devout."

I knew I had received something special in the way I felt toward everything and everyone, everywhere in the subsequent hours. The sensations lasted for hours, and I'd find myself bursting into tears at the slightest thought of acknowledgement again and again. The complete feeling of wholeness could only be described as utter tranquility. I was still feeling all the new, tearful moments of joy when again Gods voice began speaking to me and a mental conversation ensued. God, our father, Jesus, our lord, and the Holy Spirit and I spoke for many hours in regards to my journey, what I had witnessed, and how it was that I had become part of such a miraculous blessing. I felt humbled knowing that what I had experienced was from the divine, and that each of the revelations I'd gained was sacred. As our conversation concluded I found myself in perfect peace, I said goodnight and went to sleep. Over the next few days I thought about that incredible journey but I seemed to revert back to my submissive perspective of life and of my limited understanding of the moment, and what God had asked of me.

Devotion

It was truly amazing to finally grasp the omnipotent grandeur of the supernatural transit system—greatness which could only be of a divine nature. As the magnitude of my insights set in, I began to feel great affection for God and realized how amazing a creator God is. I knew that the intricacies of all we know and all we don't know, the timing of true perfection, and the scale of such wondrous beauty could only be from God. We all witness such brilliance and grace within every breath, but sometimes we do not even understand and realize the vastness of what we are truly experiencing. I had felt many emotions and had many thoughts throughout my journey of discovery, and now an even more amazing sensation was beginning to resonate from within.

Having those wondrous moments with God opened my eyes even further. I could see just how the experiences I was a part of were leading to something I couldn't yet possibly understand. I knew it was all from God, and I knew it was going to be the truth.

"For the Lord is good; his mercy is everlasting, and His truth endures to all generations" (PSALMS 100:5)

The Mist

With all that I have witnessed and with all that has come to light, I have truly realized that everything is of God's will. He allows us to be born into this world and gives us each the same potential to explore, appreciate, and admire life, which is such a glorious experience of vitality.

All our actions, every thought, every emotion, everything we have ever done, and everything we have ever been a part of, we have experienced because of God's will. The fact that we woke up today is a blessing; a gift for tomorrow is promised to no one. Every moment, from that of awakening should be looked upon as a gift, and we should learn to be truly thankful for the opportunity of life and everything in it. If you're currently not looking upon the world this way, I strongly recommend opening your eyes and your heart to the will of God. I believe I have been able to experience such intricate aspects of life because of God and his grace. All that I have accomplished and all that I have seen I owe to God, for without God's will, none of us could be.

Defining the moments

Each experience I had over the previous ten years shared many commonly occurring aspects. If I had not carefully considered them individually, I may not have comprehended the complete truth of the next observation. I found this truth to be one of the most significant, though.

> *"When anyone attempts to define a particular moment, regardless of whatever the experience may yield, he/she automatically limits its potential."*

Granted, the moment will be exactly what it is supposed to be; but we may not comprehend the experience as perhaps it could have been understood, had we not told the experience what it should or should not be. I believe this is another of God's amazing mysteries—it shows us how deep and limitless his knowledge and understanding is of all and in all.

Those insights directly led to understanding the difference between the conscious mind and a higher state of consciousness—one I truly understand and believe to be one of the foundations necessary to achieve spiritual insight and knowledge. As I mentioned before, there are many paths to acquiring such a perspective, but being prepared for what may lead to such enlightenment is of great importance. Our interpretations of any given moments could increase our awareness and understanding and perception of everything. I believe our normal state of awareness and consciousness allows us to perform our everyday tasks. It often gives one a beautiful and appealing life; however, when one opens oneself up to the limitless possibilities of God, a higher state of consciousness, and deeper level of discernment, one may gain a perspective of the real nature of the highest order of truth.

- There are many ways to obtain and recognize such a divine force. It began as an instinctive feeling for me, but recognizing the phenomena may have come to mind sooner had I been more spiritually prepared by awareness techniques beforehand.
- I believe that focus and zeal were realized when I became aware of self and it's potential. Those came about directly through meditation.
- Yoga (or tai chi) contributed to physical and spiritual flexibility, and assisted with the healing aspects of moving forward.[60] Both yoga and tai chi have healing attributes in the nature of their movements.
- I also recommend focused breathing techniques to assist with deeper levels of recognition within each moment (coming to know the knower).
- In that heightened state of consciousness, I would also recommend entering each experience, lesson, or moment in a penitent manner. I truly believe the repentance of sins, penitence, and faith in God aided me in noticing and comprehending the divine message.
- A state of Zen and enlightenment was achieved through direct intuition and spiritual growth, and initially through the direct alignment and centering of my energy points/my chakras. We tend to project our emotions and communicate using those energy signatures, and that directly affects everyone and everything, everywhere.
- We communicate at every moment with each other through energy patterns which are directly related to our emotional states.

---

60   Tai chi: A Chinese form of physical exercise characterized by a series of very slow and deliberate balletic body movements

These insightful truths are of great importance to us all and had I been more aware of their existence and how I should interact with them spiritually, I may have found the truth and acquired the path to enlightenment with less difficulty and much sooner.

Sensing joy

I noticed when we are in a cheerful state, we project it outward; it's not only visible in our physical attributes but spiritually detectable to each other through our energy patterns, which are then interpreted by our chakras. That is how joy in a room is seemingly shared by those attending. It is also how we affect all things in any given place in space and time.

Our emotional energy signatures resonate from our chakras, sending an echo that travels through the vortices in time and space. This is how a psychic and all of us, generally speaking, can walk into any given place and experience the type of emotional occurrence that has transpired there. We all sense energy in every form; some of us are extremely sensitive to all energy and we can pick up on all kinds of vibrations. Many insights come to light when a person becomes that sensitive to energy and I highly recommend practicing learning to observe such a phenomenon.

Clarity of mind

We also all possess a type of sonar system within that allows us to pick up energy's wave patterns in a sensitive way. Our emotions are distinguishable and impactful, and I now realize all energy signatures are just as interpretable to anyone crossing their path of where those who left the emotional signature did so. Interpreting such energy begins very similarly to the way a child begins to read. I could compare it to mental phonics: While a child learns to combine visual and audible signs to sound out letters, a seeker, while in a heightened state of awareness, sounds out each energy signature and learns to feel the emotional alphabet. Once we have learned to understand the fundamentals of how it works and what others' emotions feel like, we can begin to interpret between others emotional energy signatures as well.

Our thoughts and emotions are extremely important to our interactions with others in life—they carry a similar energy signature that our speech does, and are just as powerful a communication tool as words are. Being able to sense all types of energy has helped me to realize just how important it is to be a good person and generally think proper, true, and kind thoughts; and it is also an important aspect to being able to obtain a heightened state of awareness and completely understand another's audible and mental communicative interaction.

I believe we can achieve clarity of mind and attain the proper mindset by constantly remaining focused on many attributes:

By keeping good and proper thoughts and emotions.
By being selfless and kind.
By remaining filled with virtue.
By continuing in search of the truth.
By having hope, persistence, and perseverance.
By standing upright, and boldly obtaining
the path to righteousness.

Working this list into each day of life has directly contributed to my observation of a narrow path through an amazing labyrinth we know as the conscious and subconscious. It also helped to allow for the signs of life to become fully recognizable in every moment.

When I refer to the proper mindset, it is in regard to always maintaining the full awareness of each thought and emotion present in every moment. Staying positive, good and focused on God aids us in our complete and full awareness of the truth of life. For example: As I stared at a brick in the wall, I could see the visible surface but looked even further. My next realization was one of thanks—thankfulness to the painter, to the paint company, to the paint salesman, to the grout salesman, to the quarry worker, to the quarry company that developed each brick—to everyone who interacted with one another to allow the wall to contribute to such a perspective. I thought about all of that within the instant of staring at the one brick in the wall. Nothing in the wall would have been possible were it not for the will of God. When I view anything, anywhere, I can see that had it not been for God, none of what I see would be.

Everything matters

Faith, clarity, and continuously acknowledging God is the proper mindset that has allowed for such miraculous insight into much of the supernatural phenomena; it has also allowed for observations of God's perfect synchronicity of all our thoughts, emotions, and actions. He perfectly aligns everything within the material world and beyond. I have seen many moments when God's timing has been looked upon as accidental or even coincidental, and I assure you, the fact that each of us woke up today is not an accident. We should all first grasp this truthful understanding and then live with purpose on purpose. One of the amazing observances of God's perfect synchronization is seeing how we connect to others, the synchronicity that seemingly allows for interaction with those of the past or present in creative moments of transcendence. There are so many aspects to life, and each of us has a purpose and a part to contribute. Most importantly, we should be thoughtful and considerate, helping others selflessly and without expectations; hoping, helping, and praying for others well-being, especially for those who are in despair or suffering needlessly—either mentally or physically. We should always be mindful and more selfless towards everyone.

> *"Let nothing be done through selfish ambition or conceit, but in lowliness of mind let each esteem others better than himself."* (PHILIPPIANS 2:3).

At this point I began making reference to God in everything. I was in search of sanctification, and it was here on my journey that I truly began seeing God in everything–everywhere.

Transcending the arts

Another amazing aspect of God's perfect timing and synchronicity is its alignment with music and our spirit—a splendid synchronous interaction that seemingly allows those of the past or present to come together in creative moments of transcendence. Not only does God's synchronicity give us incredible insights into our spiritual lives, it uses a few different mediums, all based off the power of words, to do so. If you can't recognize such moments within your life, I strongly recommend opening your eyes and searching for anything that may seem to be missing. Follow your hunch or your instincts to become. Simply release, let go of everything within the moment, and simply be the way you are meant to always be.

JAMES MARTINEZ

I've experienced transcendence with music, as I expect many others have. One of my first observations was that transcendence can transpire not only with music, but with film and literature too. I've experienced many instances of my emotions and thoughts perfectly aligning with certain song lyrics or lines from a book. It's always put a smile on my face to realize how amazing God's creation truly is, and when I witness such a poignant aspect of life, I can also sense its connections to God's perfect synchronicity.

There is a scene early in the film *Imagine* when a man seems confused and disoriented because he was sure that the music he was hearing was accurately depicting his life.[61] The fact that he went to extremes to get some understanding (and showed up at the artist's home) was a bit disturbing; however, the man directly experienced the form of God's synchronicity that most of us connect to regularly with music. Whether it is music or film or literature, their underlying qualities include God, synchronicity, and transcendence. It's similar to a choreographed dance—without each movement in perfect synchronization with the music, it simply would not be all it is meant to be.

It holds true with all experiences of creativity—they are moments of affirmation when we can truly see that we all connect to one another. Many great authors can transcend enough to accurately depict another's complete life—their characters' thoughts, emotions, and life experiences can merge in perfect alignment with the reader's. The experiences are part of God's perfect synchronicity, and they become apparent when readers fully live in those moments (that is after they've attained the proper mindset and higher state of awareness to observe them). Powerful

61   John Lennon is talking to a young man at his mansion in Tittenhurst Park, Ascot, on Saturday May 22nd, 1971. http://www.youtube.com/watch?v=qUUvw-kOPtQ

emotions become a medium in time and space (unless one still has reason to believe in coincidences).

Film also shares actions and emotions across space and time. Our emotions allow us to feel as if we are a part of the story being told. Empathy allows us to become connected to the movie's story line and, once again, it is based off of the power of words. Once space and time are factored into the equation, it becomes an even more complex occurrence, because there is a brief interaction across space and time that assists in our ability to connect to the actor's emotional content directly in front of us. This interaction comes from one's internal emotional energy; it resonates from our chakras or chi and then instantly travels a vortex or temporal nexus to its destination. It is how we are able to connect emotionally with something such as film.

I now understand our energy to be one of the essentials of this complex world; it allows us to communicate, even across space and time, with another's emotions. I also understand the interactions of energy are in place so that we may better grasp each moment of emotional unity between each other. As we mature, our overall perspective changes; our emotional responses also change slightly, and thus give new meaning to a once-familiar emotion or thought. It is how we can hear any old song, read an old book or see an old film and add an additional transcendental viewpoint to those we once had.

The artist responsible for creating music writes emotional content that we can relate to. When our senses connect with an appealing song, we tend to gain another emotional attribute and perspective that synchronizes or unties us. We then become conscious of the moment while our emotions and thoughts interact, in however brief an interlude, across the boundaries of space and time.

The creative mediums of literature, film and music are all based off the power of words and pictures, and are completely interwoven with everyone, everywhere. They provide a creative conduit that helps us become aware of each moment, and of how we fit together, in order to recognize our moments of connectivity, it's a brief transcendent interaction. Every aspect of our everyday lives is synchronized—something we see much more easily when we reach a higher state of awareness. It's then recognizable due to our higher vantage point and perceptions of life and relationships. I compare it to the intricacies of a labyrinth—from the ground level, each wall seems to look the same to us and we are unaware of each path's direction; however, when our vantage point changes and allows for a more complete view of the labyrinth, we gain the ability to see its beginning and its end and all the paths in between. We now have the vantage point needed to comprehend the interwoven complexities of the beautiful world and our actions within it.

Affecting our surroundings

I could recognize the sense of God's perfect timing and tapestry in every moment. I could see that my actions and thoughts were in synchronization with every step within my life. I had reached another milestone in understanding, and had become so sensitive to every aspect of my surroundings that I felt as if I had a direct and instant effect on my environment—I could make inexplicable moments come to fruition just by thinking about them. I realize powers such as those could be judged, however, the extents of the abilities were limited to observational ones, and could not be used for personal gain. For example, a severe thunderstorm had blown in one evening and I was admiring the permeating crackle of thunder as the lightening snapped through the night sky. After hearing one lightning bolt strike, I thought I would really enjoy seeing a bolt of lightning actually strike. At that exact moment I walked to my kitchen window, pulled the drawstring and, just as the blinds reached the top of the windowsill, a bolt of lightning came down right in the center of the window's view and within a half of mile of my house. I was in complete awe; I felt attuned with everything, with all my surroundings, and with each breath. *All thanks to God.*

Visiting a special place

I started another evening with my usual preparations, and when I began to reach the summit of energy and awareness, I noticed the tiny particles of energy I've previously described. They reminded me of many tiny snowflakes falling to the ground, and their incessant shine captivated my attention. As they flowed faster and faster in unison, from top to bottom, I watched them form a single line, rotate three times, and I entered a vortex with them. The cylindrical-shaped tunnel was brightly lit. It was perfect in circumference; there were intricate workings and defining characteristics from section to section, and they all connected smoothly and seamlessly. Each main section of the celestial tunnel or transit system connected to the one before and the one after it. The light seemed to flow through interwoven fibers, something reminiscent to what I have seen of woven nano-stitching.

As I navigated the tunnel I paid careful attention to how it all was happening. I noticed I was swirling, turning, swaying, and moving in bending directions from left to right and up and down, as if I was on a roller coaster ride. I then arrived at a meeting place where hundreds to thousands of angels were milling about freely and purposefully in any given room, each of which appeared to connect to another room through endless interconnecting passageways. The rooms were of different configurations than a typical four-walled structure. Each room had different levels and heights and proportions than the one before and after it. I could see no visible ceiling and the walls had no end, yet I could not see a sky. Some of the other rooms were storied between other rooms and were connected by stairwells and walkways. I noticed some walls were curved as I moved by and transitioned from one room to the next.

Although many of the celestial beings had congregated in some areas, many others were on the move with an important task to complete. All the hallways led into other rooms completely filled with many more angels. Sometimes the areas were large, larger than twenty thousand square feet, whereas other rooms were the size of a small house. Despite the lack of visible electrical lighting, a distinct luminescent lighting gave the walls and surrounding areas an interesting glow.

I moved closer to one of the stairwells and wondered which way I would go. As soon as I thought about going up, I began to go up. I would simply think of a direction and I would move in it. As I moved on stairwells to different rooms and from area to area, I directly approached the supernatural beings that would move away from me in the most peculiar way—they would turn and begin to move in a way unlike any human movement. It seemed as if we were not supposed to clearly see one another. Again, their movements resembled a person running at fast speeds, but their steps made it look as if they were running in place. As soon as I stopped gazing directly upon them, they would turn towards me once again and begin to move back toward me in a normal walking manner. I finally recognized them to be the same supernatural beings that I had seen in my peripheral vision, the ones I previously described as being flat or distorted and who I believed to be in a constant state of dance and movement.

As the night progressed and my observations continued, I noticed that some of the celestial beings had the characteristics of males while others clearly had the characteristics of females. They all moved about with vigor and copious amounts of energy, however, I could not determine if the rooms I observed them in were simply common areas or if they congregated there at all times. Our communication came in the form of telepathy, and they seemed to be just as intrigued with my being there as I was.

I noticed an oval-shaped stage in one of the rooms, nearly three feet tall with several steps that fronted it. It appeared to be approximately one hundred and fifty feet in circumference. Groups of beings moved about and moved closer to the stage, and within ten to twenty seconds of stepping onto the platform, they suddenly transformed from their original appearance into a fine mist of energy particles. They then appeared to be transported to another place altogether because they disappeared. I saw something hanging directly above the stage—it was one of the starting points the supernatural beings had been coming from all the while. It resembled a large tubular venting shaft bending along a ceiling and then leading upward, and I asked one of the angels what it was. I was told it was a way for them to navigate to and from locations. When I asked how it worked, I was told that only God knows exactly how it works. I thought back to how I had seen the supernatural beings transform from an astral body to a fine mist of particles of energy, and I was now witnessing it (similar to how I understood an atomizer to work).

I witnessed the occurrence several more times and then decided that I would like to explore the system more closely, and personally travel on it. Before I knew it, I found myself moving over and onto the passageway on the stage. I looked around and saw many of the celestial beings completely surrounding me. Then I felt something coming down from overhead and as the temperature and climate changed, I could feel moisture reach my face and then my arms. The air had a lot of precipitation in it; it felt like water but smelt and tasted like a mixture of something I have not tasted or smelt before or since. It had to be a special type of substance that assisted in the transformation process. It felt like I was standing in the midst of a waterfall and then, before I knew it, the view I had of the room I was in changed and the supernatural beings began to step off the platform. It was instantaneous; the room changed right before my eyes. I had traveled into another room within that incredible place via that delivery platform. I was completely enthralled.

I observed the celestial beings for a great portion of that night, moving from room to room and learning to navigate around their remarkable network of interconnecting passageways and areas, meeting and greeting many of the angels. As I stood before a group of them, I realized I had been observing that otherworldly realm for a long period of time. I decided to conclude that remarkable journey and began to think of my home. I focused on one of the angels and seemed to have the experience I had witnessed one of the angels have—I appeared to transcend back to my home in the material world—and I could see the transition from point A in the otherworldly spiritual realm to point B in my home. The otherworldly location seemed to stretch in an infinite manner while I arrived back home, and I realized that I was still fixated on one of the angels that was standing in direct proximity to me while I was at their location. I had spiritually arrived back at my home instantly, but the process appeared to take place extremely slow. Amazingly, I could physically see the angel taking on a physical form and physically arriving with me. It was as if I had, by thought, brought the otherworldly being with me. Then suddenly, as if reality would not allow for it, the celestial being began to atomize and assimilate into my immediate surroundings, into the background, and then vanish altogether. The entire transition back was simply a matter of seconds. Completely awake, I sat up and meditated on all I had witnessed. I understood every detail of every event that became knowledge and an intricate aspect of my life was because of God.

God is amazing

I firmly believe that with God, the task in front of us is never as great as the power behind us—a belief that has aided me along my journey of self-discovery. We live in a world within a world within a world—a place where our dreams bring our deepest concerns to resolution and our hopes and expectations to fruition. (I believe) we visit similar places to those nightly as we transcend while we sleep. Our spirit, conscious and subconscious minds enigmatically connect, through the closest vortex, to the mystical, sacred, and spiritual realm in all of our lives. I believe it exists to aid us along our paths of life and to also direct us to our paths after life.

Know that everything has a reason and purpose. So when we dismiss the signs of life before us, we automatically deny integral aspects to our lives; we then begin limiting our capabilities. Recognizing the signs, understanding them, and then acting upon them are very important. While we are all capable of great things, I believe that having faith and trust in God is the most significant great thing we can do, for without God, none of us could be.

Transcendence

As the supernatural phenomena continued to occur, I was beginning to (audibly) hear the many angels arriving and departing. I could not always see when it happened though, but I noticed an energy signature that came in the form of a sound. The sudden appearance of a being's presence sounded like one solid object instantly tapping against another solid object. Sometimes the sound was loud, at other times it was extremely faint, or sometimes I could just see the fast moving blur, but usually their arrival and departure was recognizable. Little did I know that that discovery was merely the eve of something even more wonderful—an experience that I can say, with all my heart, has been one of the greatest moments of my life.

A unique being

I was lying in bed one Saturday evening, meditating and listening to music on the radio. A female artist, who was also a spiritual leader, was playing "religious folk music" and the music was rather amazing. I had listened to that radio station often but could not recall that particular genre being its mainstay. I could sense something inside the moment was distinctive but I could not quite determine what it was, so I began to prepare myself spiritually. Just as I reach alignment, I was filled with an inner peace and I reached the pinnacle of my perceptions, I found myself radiating a bright bluish-white fluorescent light again that seemed to shine from within. I noticed I was also hovering spiritually about twenty feet off the ground. I could see another being there with me, and I felt the location I was in was associated with divine power and that I should hold the meeting in high regard.

I could clearly see another being standing below and to the left of where I was hovering. I had been finding that when in an enlightened perspective, it enhanced my point of view, and with that more passive perspective, I could see that the remarkable being had a very unique presence. Its entire skin color was blue—a blue like the color of the sky filled with water before a rainstorm. Then the marvelous being extended itself by its neck and stretched its head in an upward direction until it reached my feet; then it began to swirl around my body very slowly, as to observe every aspect of me from every angle. It then reached my direct line of sight and I could see it in great detail, despite its body still standing about twenty feet below mine. It had a bovine head—one very similar to that of an ox or a cow. I knew I had already attained enlightenment by the blue-white glow emanating from within, and I had a strong feeling of peace in its presence, and my first expressed thought was about how beautiful I thought the being to be. I then came to understand I was in the presence of an extraordinary spiritual being. I continued to feel meek and calm and was consenting passively to each moment; I was hoping to truly comprehend my place and the magnitude of such an encounter. When suddenly I began to hear a voice, it was loud and clear and distinct.

Do you believe?

I was asked,

"Do you believe that Jesus Christ is the Son of God?"

My response was, "Yes, I believe that Jesus Christ is the Son of God. He is Lord and Savior!"

Instantly I knew everything was different, I felt I was in a holy place, and I changed my physical position on my bed from lying down to kneeling. I then leaned forward over my knees and I could feel the inherent emotional warmth of the encounter. I began to pray and give thanks to God for several minutes, and then as I sat up, my viewpoint had suddenly changed: I found myself kneeling in an otherworldly place altogether.

> *"Enter into his gates with thanksgiving, and into his courts with praise. Be thankful to Him; bless His name."* (PSALM 100:4)

In his presence

My eyes were suddenly allowed to see that I was kneeling in a sunken portion of an outdoor courtyard. I could feel the majesty and the all-powerful divine all around. I could see stars twinkling in the sky up above, and I could see it was both day and night; I could instantly see everything I gazed upon, however, I could not see a brightness reminiscent to our sun's. God's light allowed for everything within this place to be visible. I then noticed several steps slightly in front of me, and at the top of them sat the presence of excellence. Amazingly I was being blessed with the incredible opportunity to see God in his realm of glory, and the realization instantly humbled me beyond measure. I could tell that I was in God's court; it was filled with my wonder and his holiness.

As curious as I always am, I wondered where the supreme location could be, but then I realized there could only be one place and that is wherever God says it is. I knew it was a heavenly realm. I turned my head to look around the area of which I knelt. I could see several pillars on each of the corners of the courtyard holding up a pergola, and I could see what appeared to be a tabernacle directly behind God. I began to slowly turn my head to see what was behind me and just as I looked to the left, I heard an amazing voice say,

"Don't turn your back on me."

I didn't, but I could see a large pyramid just inside the left corner of my peripheral vision. It stood in the far distance, at the end of what appeared to be a long stretch of garden with many trees on both sides, and it seemed to be several hundred feet high.

Finding God

I was introduced to seven unique beings sitting under the pergola. They all sat in very distinct seats; a few of them reminded me of a chase lounge, while others resembled artistic chairs with carvings along the arm rests. I understood them all to be seraphim, each one sat observing me and engaging me in conversation—there were two to the left, two to the right, and three in front— each sat in a unique place in the court. As I began to comprehend what I was doing there I said,

"You found me."

And God said, "You found me."

Thinking now about the importance and truth of his words, I believe that although we are all born into God's marvelous earth, we must individually seek God and come to understand that only a path of love and righteousness can lead to God.

I had been kneeling for some time in a penitent manner, all the time aware of the magic and marvel of where I was, I felt as if another person was directly pressing underneath both of my palms. We all spoke kindly to one another, and while the touch on my palms continued to move in a slow swirling circular motion, our gracious conversations carried on about a great many things. I was asked about myself, who I thought I was and how I felt about experiencing the many spiritual insights which were recently coming to light. I spoke truthfully and boldly about what I had found, what I had learned, and how I had learned it.

After several hours of conversation our meeting concluded and I suddenly found myself in another place altogether. I realized the incredible sensation I was feeling was that of the vortices spinning on my palms, and then suddenly I noticed I was no longer kneeling before the majesty of God.

A new days dawn

I looked around and noted it was extremely dark out, yet there was a peaceful serenity encompassing the moment. Off in the far distance, a sliver of light became visible. I witnessed the sky slowly change colors from a dark black to dark blue to gray to white to magenta and then to light blue. In the far backdrop of where we stood was a colossal cloud formation. Light began to slowly peek through one of the clouds. The area beneath me then appeared to reflect the light coming through from up above.

I detected a slight sound and a faint smell of water, and then I noticed water was all around us . . . I realized then I was in the middle of the ocean at daybreak with God, the father of all creation. The wind was gently blowing about, and the water sounded as if another had waved his hand slowly across its still surface.

God's voice is ever so gentle and amazing, and every time he spoke and prepared me for a new scene, I felt at complete peace. I spoke with God about his beauty and his marvelous assault on my senses. Initially I could only manage to utter the words *beautiful* and *amazing*. I thought that of the beautiful sky and the amazing cloud formations that he was showing me, when the topic of how much I loved and appreciated the beach arose. I contemplated all the beauty before me and then, yet again, I was miraculously and instantly somewhere else. We had moved somewhere else entirely and when I became curious as to where we were, God said,

"Be patient and prepare yourself."

An ocean garden

I first noticed the change in the atmosphere and in my immediate surroundings. My next observation was of the air— it was highly saturated with moisture and I could feel it on the skin of my face and arms. I could not see where I was standing; I could not even see my hand right before my face. Then I thought to God, *Where am I, and what is this place?*

God said, "Get ready"...then paused for fifteen seconds and said, "Okay here it comes...now."

We stood very near a beach and then I began to recognize the familiarities of being that close to the ocean. At God's command the mist and fog slowly began to retreat in a uniformed line. I could hear the waves breaking nearby, so I looked over the edge of the hill to see the ocean waves. They were crashing onto a beautiful beach which appeared to be less than a hundred yards from my position. The atmosphere of the place was reminiscent of the regal, all-powerful, and supreme court we were in previously. Once again it appeared to be both daytime and nighttime; everything was miraculously illuminated by the light of God. I observed the waves breaking for a while longer until I noticed a beautiful garden nearby then God said, *Take a walk with me,* and then we began to make our way over to it.

I asked God, "Where is this place?"

And God said, "This is your place."

I was not sure if he was referring to the hilltop or to the garden, perhaps both. Either way, I felt peace and tranquility as we moved through the garden on its sloping path. The ten-foot-wide path was made of perfectly laid stones, and to its left was a beautiful field of green grass. After several more steps, a picturesque rectangular fountain, full of clear water, came into view, and it appeared to be made from the same white stones we walked upon.

I continued walking and talking with God about many truths in my life. I could see more green grass and multiple colors and varieties of flowers and fountains alongside the path we were on, and as we walked around the rolling hillside, it dawned on me that we had moved from a sacred temple in his court through the wondrous beauty and stillness somewhere in the middle of the ocean, to this very instant and into this incredible walk in one of the most beautiful gardens I had ever seen.

The overlook

The path began to head back toward the ocean. We passed a few more of the spectacular fountains, each one similar in shape and size only more artistic than the one before it.

I could once again hear the waves breaking on the beach nearby, and the path led us directly to a sitting area on the top of a soft incline which overlooked the ocean (and the beach). A circular bench lined the entire circumference of the area and there was an inlet of water just behind it, and I could tell it was a special and tranquil sitting spot. God dressed in amazing attire reminiscent of something praetorian only without the head gear, walked from my side and sat down on the circular bench right before me and said to me,

"You know my son, Jesus."

Jesus also appeared at my side, walked over, and sat down next to God, our father. Jesus was dressed in a white robe and looked the way he is. Amazing with his brownish red hair, shoulder length and the exact profile I always thought him to have. I felt wonderful and peaceful, gracious and glorious and they both began to speak to me of many truths for a long period of time. We spoke of the path I had walked; we spoke of my understandings before that moment and how I then felt being in their presence; we spoke of spiritual beliefs, practices and understanding, and I shared many stories of my life. There was an incredible peace throughout the conversation. I was told many truths about myself and my journey and what was expected of me. As we spoke of my perceptions of spirituality and of my spiritual beliefs, I began to understand why and how I had arrived at that life-giving meeting. I spoke in a truthful way, describing why I believed my spiritual union with the divine had happened at that moment. This meeting lasted for several hours and then concluded upon me learning of just how incredible this journey had become.

I believe and I have faith in God, the father of all creation. I give thankfulness and praise to Jesus Christ, my Lord and Savior. This I hold in the highest regard.

A lasting fragrance

I found myself back at home almost as soon as I tried to gain perspective on what was happening. I was once again on my bed. I felt complete serenity thinking about what I had just witnessed and experienced.

When I got up and moved about, I felt as if I could feel or sense forever. I felt calm, joyful and assured. I could see that morning had just arrived, yet I felt completely rested, and then I noticed the unique fragrance of what can only be compared to freshly blooming rose petals filling the air. I could smell a wonderful and sweet fragrance throughout each room of my house for the next several days.

As I pondered the key perceptions of my incredible journey, I thought about the narrow path I'd followed, my spiritual beliefs and my mystical awareness; and I came to a realization that had it not been for God, and the culmination and combination of spiritual insights and spiritual knowledge, I would not have arrived at that miraculous moment.

Sheer beauty with God

I anticipated my next experience would be soon so I fasted for several days in preparation. I began that evening with repentance for all my misdeeds, an awareness of God's greatness, and praise. I utilized all the same focused methods that like before aided me and enabled a meeting such as this to become realized.

Inside I felt as if I was already in the presence of the Almighty. Then suddenly I felt the sensation, once again, of another being pressing the palms of my hands in very slow, continuous, swirling movements, when suddenly I found myself flying among the mountaintops. I was traveling at a moderate-enough speed, and could inspect the landscape just several feet below. I passed many small brush trees, and then a beautiful waterfall towering hundreds of feet above a body of water, it was flowing over rugged rock formations. The rocks were in earth tones, mostly dark and light brown with some jagged, flat, and smooth edges. I cleared the mountains and then I could see homes along the next mountain's ridgeline. They stretched along the top of the ridge and down towards the large body of water I was flying over. I floated toward the water level, directly towards a home on stilts that had a stairwell that connected to a wooden deck under the house. It was a gorgeous day; I could feel the wind blowing and I could smell the moisture in the air. God and I made our way down the stairs of the deck and into the water. I could feel myself floating in the waves as they swayed back and forth. I spoke to God about how the house reminded me of a home I had dreamt of several nights earlier—in it, I transcended to a home at the base of a thousand-foot waterfall—with water falling from atop the ridge of a nearby mountain and landing on the deck. I noted how I was in a similar experience with God, our father. I knew that I had had a premonition of that event and now I was experiencing its déjà vu.

God didn't comment on my observations, but told me that it was a place he had not been to in some time. Then he expressed how beautiful a location it was. Situated in the middle of a large body of water with rugged mountains on all sides and an amazing waterfall off in the distance, what was there not to love and appreciate about that special place? We spoke for a while longer about its beauty and then as I gazed upon the hillside, my understanding changed, and suddenly the beautiful hills just near a beach began to change and reform when my emotional perspective had changed. I started to lose focus, fear and doubt arose within, and in an instant the entire landscape had changed. It transformed into a completely different landscape altogether. I began to feel bad about what I had just done, I knew this was because God had just expressed how beautiful this place is and then he told me not to worry about it he would fix it. I believe it was a lesson on how to remain positive and focused onto God. I would later find out the significance of that meeting and the importance of staying focused on God.

In another instant we left that place, and for a brief moment I thought I was back in my room, but there was a view out of a window which overlooked the ocean. I could see a picturesque backdrop of the clouds and the ocean which appeared to indicate that sunset was near. The colors were vibrant and stunning. I thought *This is what loveliness must truly mean* and all I could seem to say was, "Beautiful" over and over. As incredibly serene and delightful as all the exquisiteness truly was, I could only utter two or three words. Of course it was beautiful, but taking in so much beauty and grandeur was too overwhelming to describe in just one breath. God had instantly moved us to another place for a special purpose.

An important question

In this next meeting with God, the father of all creation, and Jesus Christ, His Son, we sat in the room overlooking that incredible sunset. We spoke again of spirituality and of religion. We spoke of different happenings and belief systems. We spoke of devoutness, piety, and godliness. We spoke more of writing down the details of what I had experienced and of my spiritual beliefs. I told them that

I had hoped to write a manuscript that I believed would describe my wonderful beliefs and experiences. God, our father, and Jesus then asked me a very important question. God asked,

"What is your opinion of the Bible?"

Almost immediately I replied, "I don't think it's needed."

Instantly I heard someone say, "That's blasphemy."

I was not sure why or how that was of significance but I made note and then said that I was not sure of what to write, how to do it, or where to begin. Truthfully I didn't know how to respond to God when he asked my thoughts of the bible. I honestly thought with what I had been experiencing and become a part of that I could write something that would be as beneficial to those in need of finding God or finding a way to understand the word of God.

God and Jesus began to speak to one another about something; I could tell they were planning something important.

God then asked,

"Can you write a manuscript?"

I replied, "Yes, I can. I can do it." Pointing to my left and right arms and saying aloud, "With persistence and perseverance right here I can do anything."

Then God said, "Okay I'm going to let you write it. It's not going to be easy but I will be right there with you. Start at the beginning and keep it simple and direct."

And before God, our father, and Jesus His son, I agreed to write a manuscript describing my understandings, beliefs, and truthful thoughts on life and spirituality. I knew the message would encompass all I had witnessed, all that I had learned and been a part of.

God then asked,

"How do you plan on writing the manuscript and what do you plan to say?"

I knew nothing about writing a manuscript. I did not know what I would say or where I would begin, but once I accepted the assignment, God told me I would start at the beginning and tell my story from there. I knew I could do it. God gave me the first line and the last line of the manuscript and told me I would have the rest of the story. God is incredible and amazing, and Jesus is wonderful and supreme, and their divinity together was sublime. Every extra moment with them gave me clear insight into reverence, truth, holiness, peace, and sanctity. I spoke with them truthfully in every moment. I drank in the mountainside, the ocean view, the horizon of such a startlingly and spectacular creation, and began to feel a strange sensation come over me. It seemed familiar to the previous one that indicated a change of location was coming, only without the peculiar swirling motions underneath my palms. Everything suddenly and miraculously changed right before my eyes.

God's waterfall

Instantly I found myself in an atrium or foyer, and I felt utter tranquility. I could not have imagined such a special place existed had I not been there to see its grandeur and majesty firsthand. Peacefulness and holy vitality were everywhere, it had an astounding atmosphere I recognized from the regal courtyard and from the hilly overlook. The feelings of comfort and absolute peace were fully evident; the magnificent place lacked nothing. I was inside a structure unlike anything equal in design or construction. What surprised me most of all was the amazing energy that was present in every direction, similar to the energy I had been feeling beneath my palms. The energy form came from many evenly shaped symmetrical vortices. Each vortex was several millimeters in diameter and had a bluish white glow and a sparkle. The twinkles coming from each of the vortices placed throughout every space had a distinct purpose, I could see this was truly Gods creation.

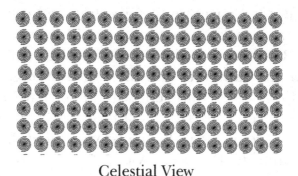

Celestial View

Just in front and to the left of where we stood was a large dining area, with a table thirty feet long and with chairs along both sides and one on each end. I could see another room in the distance just on the other side of the dining table with no visible door. Its entrance was the size of the entire room (the entrance which measured about forty feet wide and ten feet high). I could not see where the room led to, but the area to the right of its right wall rose up into a majestic, opened larger section of the atrium. As I looked up into the grand area I could see water from a hundred-foot-tall waterfall, falling in that opened section. The water that fell over its edge formed droplets which slowly fell onto a large rock formation beneath—three large rocks perfectly placed upon one another and surrounded by a water collection area underneath it. The only sound within this wondrous place was of water droplets splashing and gracefully landing on the rocks.

God's place

To the right of the waterfall I saw another simple yet glorious room which had a row of windows that stretched down its length.

I asked God, "Where is this place?"

God said, "This is a special place; no one else has ever been here before." And then God said, "This is my place."

I was mesmerized and thankful for having been taken there. In the beautiful calmness I could still see the symmetrical vortices all around—sparkling rings within rings leading to a central glow which seemed to resonate and travel back to the outermost ring. I was curious about the sparkling points of energy. Then I noticed there was a path which led from where we stood around where the water fell, and it passed alongside the long row of windows. As we walked along this path God began to show me around his flawless sanctuary. We made our way through several rooms and by his office into another magnificent room with a large section for sitting. We sat and God and I then began to speak about many things, we spoke about his place, his creations, this meeting and many wondrous and beautiful truths and suddenly images of real places and far off locations began to appear right before my eyes simply by God having thought of them. It happened directly as we gazed upon an area—every vortex twinkled and another location became visible right behind them, just like a picture screen. He showed great views and amazing places. He showed an incredible palace that had a brilliant sparkle, he told me it was his shiny palace. We spoke peacefully and as we talked the entire place we sat in began to twinkle and glimmer. He told me I was the first to notice the vortex in such a way.

Blasphemy

As we continued talking for a while longer, I was asked many questions and I asked many questions. We spoke of how beautiful his place is and how wonderful everything is. Suddenly I had an inappropriate thought and God said,

"That's blasphemy; ask for forgiveness."[62]

I immediately asked God for forgiveness and God forgave me. I was instantly experiencing humility. The conversation ensued again and I did it again, I blasphemed. I thought of the same thought I had just asked God to forgive me for and again God said, "That's blasphemy, ask for forgiveness."

I immediately asked God for forgiveness and God forgave me again. I was hoping to understand what was happening, because I often think and rethink situations and moments, yet once again I blasphemed before God and God said,

"That's blasphemy, ask for my forgiveness."

I said, "God, I'm sorry for my blasphemy, will you please forgive me?"

And God forgave me. What was surprising to me was knowing that I was in the presence of God, the father of all creation, and yet I could not seem to bridal my thoughts. I asked God,

"How is it that can I still be here with you, in your presence, after I blasphemed and behaved in that way?"

And God said, "There is a judgment day for all of us."

I was amazed with God's grandeur, beauty, and grace, and with how understanding he is towards everything. Then God helped me to better understand what I was doing, what I had learned, and how to move forward through the experience. He told me not to worry and to have faith and to stay focused onto him.

---

62   Blasphemy: Something done or said that shows disrespect for God or sacred things

Grace

Then God asked,

"What do you plan on titling the manuscript?"

I thought about it for a moment and then spoke a title. It didn't even seem fitting so I spoke another title, and that appeared to be incorrect also. I thought of another and spoke it and it, too, seemed unsuitable. I thought again of another title and it appeared to also be inadequate. It continued again and again, and my inability to answer God's question precisely became evident.

As I continued to respond in such a way for several moments, I noticed our location changed from his beautiful and peaceful sanctuary back to the room with a view overlooking a beautiful ocean. It was the room that I was conversing with God and Jesus in beforehand. *Wow, what a truly wonderful expression of grace*, I thought.

> *"So I have looked for You in the sanctuary,*
> *To see Your power and Your glory. Because*
> *Your lovingkindness is better than life, My*
> *lips shall praise You."* (PSALMS 63:2-3).

I was once again in the room overlooking the ocean before God and Jesus. A feeling of confidence engulfed me and a smile crossed my face. We spoke more of the manuscript and of its delivery. I was again asked how long it would take for me to complete it, and not having written a manuscript before on anything, let alone something as detailed as the observance of transcendence with God, our father. I was feeling extremely bold and fearless in every emotional sense, and I thought about how every single thing that had happened to me was because of God's will and God's grace, then I spoke out,

"Six months."

God pointed out that Jesus wrote a manuscript in forty days.

Then I said, "Four months."

I was reminded, once again, of the importance of the task. I was to bring another perspective to any who might be experiencing difficulty understanding our journey in life.

I found myself once again in my room, full of hopeful thoughts about properly interpreting everything I had just experienced. I could once again smell the sweet fragrance of newly blossomed rose petals in the air, and I realized I was still in the presence of God, the father, the Son, and several angels who were encompassing God.

I had an unbridled thought and was immediately confronted by one of the angels. As I asked God for forgiveness and said that I was sorry, and immediately the angel moved back from me. God forgave me and I was feeling many emotions and experiencing many confusing thoughts. I felt humble, yet for some unknown reason I could not keep myself from sometimes thinking inappropriate and even blasphemous thoughts. God knew what I was in need of, and I prayed to God for his help. I asked him to cleanse me. I was then confronted with an ethereal and sacred being, the beautiful Holy Spirit, and as I gazed upon her, God spoke to me and began to inform me of what was now happening to me. I could see how beautiful the Holy Spirit truly is and how gracefully she moved. She stood before me with several unique beings directly behind her. Here grace and beauty, unparallel to anyone I'd ever seen. As she stood before me fearless I could see her gazing at something deep inside of me.

Spiritual cleansing

I thought back to when I had prayed to God for a better way of expressing myself. He had answered that prayer then and yet every now and again I had a profane thought in a way I could not understand and did not want. We spoke for several moments about this, and once again I asked to be cleansed of my sins and to be absolved of my inability to not think loving and pure thoughts always. I realized I was in the presence of the Holy Trinity and then I felt the power of the Holy Spirit, when she reach into me and grab hold of something that was within, and I saw the Holy Spirit's hands pull it out of me. I could not make out clearly what was being removed, but I understand now that I was being spiritually cleansed by the Holy Spirit while God and Jesus witnessed it. The experience lasted for several minutes, and each time the Holy Spirit reached into me I began to use profanity. She graciously grabbed hold of that which was causing the unwarranted outbursts of profanity. I abhorred the outbursts and yet they seemingly clung to me, but with each pass of deliverance, I felt a load lifted and breathed a bit easier. It was as if the unwarranted sin was kicking and screaming as it left my body, but eventually over several passes I could feel a sense of ease, grace, and cleanliness. It spread throughout my entire body and spirit as goodwill encompassed me. As these humbling moments concluded, I completely felt as if I were a newborn, humble and at peace with everything and with everyone. I was in a perfect state of Zen, bliss, penitence, and grace all at once, and I accepted every moment of life completely and thankfully. This was the first time I had ever known this kind of peace and tranquility truly exists. I thank you God, I thank you Jesus, and I thank you Holy Spirit for cleansing me in that amazing way.

Another look at heaven

There I lay in bed, magnificently cleansed by the Holy Spirit, when I once again felt the power of the Holy Trinity.

I was at complete peace with God, and then instantly we transcended. We were somewhere else and I was being shown around another incredible place. I was mesmerized and in awe with all I could see. The outdoor place we were at was filled with astounding grandeur; a beautiful place with undulating hills lined with green grassy clothing; trees in full perfect foliage which grew exactly where they were supposed to, and even perfectly separated from one another; yawning meadows at the feet of the hills, gently buffering a stream that flowed easily between them. The place was but one small perfect part of his infinite beautiful kingdom. The grounds all appeared to be perfectly groomed, and not yet knowing where I was I asked God,

"Is this a golf course or something?"

God immediately replied, "No, it is not. This is a special place."

God then led me into open pastures as green as I had ever seen by way of a gold and winding road, as we passed many others who moved about with complete happiness— undisturbed and blissful within that existence. I knew that there was no want for anything there; everything one could imagine needing would instantly become available, and I witnessed that happen numerous times. Those in this place were all having the best times, they were all filled with joy and happiness. Doing wondrous things in every direction, all being loved by and loving God.

I knew God's existence is eternal and as he showed me around his kingdom of heaven I could clearly see what forever is like, and what it would be like having everything I could ever imagine forever. That helped to place back into perspective just how special and important our time on earth truly is. We are all born into existence and, God willing, we make our way to another entirely wonderful existence—to live out eternity in heaven near God.

We then entered into and moved about God's shiny palace for a while longer. I could see his palace was incredible and filled with so many beautiful rooms. I moved about with him for a while longer as he showed me around and then as our journey concluded we instantly returned home. Upon arriving back I noticed it was early morning, and I realized I had been gone all night. I thought perhaps it could have all been a dream, and then I thought about the sweet smelling fragrance which was still present throughout the house and in every inhalation. (The scent lasted for several days in the house.) I thought again about the ever-present celestial beings. I could still see vortices everywhere, even when I closed my eyes. I could see through the windows, the walls, everything. Being in God's realm was so great that I simply could not yet wrap my head around the fact that it all had just happened. Then I noticed God, our father, and Jesus Christ, and the Holy Spirit with me . . . still with me . . . and the four of us engaged in more great conversation. We spoke of how special the experience was and how good it felt to be good, this went on for several hours until it came to an end. My wonderful and spiritual holy union with the divine registered internally.

I humbly thanked God, Jesus, and the Holy Spirit for being part of such an incredible experience and then began my day. I walked into the kitchen, sat at my office desk, and I thought to myself,

How am I going to do this?

How am I going to write this manuscript?

The very instant that thought transpired, my phone vibrated and rang. I reached for the phone in puzzled amazement and noticed there was a text message which read, *Keep it simple and direct.* My mouth open briefly and I immediately began to smile. I thought to God right away about how amazing that was and I knew then He was always there.

Symmetry

It took me several more months to fully understand the magnitude of such an encounter and wondrous meeting and to place into perspective what I had been witness to and what had actually transpired. I thought again of the precise points of energy that were apparent in each location—how each symmetrical point resonated outwardly from its center, toward its outer rings, similar to how when in a glass, the water's ripple resonates outward. The force of energy that vibrates towards the outer circumference of the glass shows the movement of its energy in each wave, just like each vortex I had noticed. Each energy point was separated by only a few inches, and spaced evenly in every direction, everywhere and always. It seemed the more that I compared what I saw to natural occurrences, the more it began to make better sense to me and give me a more complete perspective.

Alignment

The vortices' symmetrical points of energy help the supernatural beings travel from other spiritual realms to our material world for whatever purpose they may have in the moment. Because their arrivals and departures directly coincide with our emotions and thoughts, it's evident we all work in unison with spiritual beings as part of the experience of life. Our paths and decisions help to shape and create the world we know.

I found this truth thanks to God and I hoped that I would be able to fully understand the lessons as they were now becoming even more difficult to grasp as I continued moving forward.

Abasement and Humility

I began searching for the common occurrences within each moment of feeling and emotion in my past that had led me to God. I asked God why it was that I did not have that kind of relationship I'd grown into with him before. I had always believed in God and I had always been raised with faith. I had often gone to church and felt God's presence in everything, yet those moments lacked the type of intimate relationship I now had with him. I felt I needed to have a better understanding of why each moment of my early existence did not allow for God to be as visible to me as he was now. God helped me to realize that he is ever present in all that he creates, in every moment forever and always. It was with that understanding that he truly helped me to move forward. He had always been with me, but I had not fully understood how to have this type of relationship yet.

I was in need of learning that truth and still in need of understanding what each lesson was truly for.

Self

I searched my whole life experiences for the complete opposite of the thoughts I now have, and emotions I now feel about God and life. That led me to see that nearly all of the early (and sometimes difficult) lessons of my life shared one common aspect—I had placed me, myself, and I first in each moment; whereas now I had God first and above me in every thought and emotion. I wondered if it could have been that I could not see God simply because I had been consumed with self, consumed with each of the moments I thought I controlled something or everything. Then I wondered if others cannot feel or see God because of their preoccupancy with self in the moment or was it perhaps their lack of understanding what God was asking of them?

I focused my attention on some of the great moments within my life when I had achieved something wonderful, and I noticed that in the midst of each moment, my appreciation and acknowledgement of God was acute. The closer I looked at what each moment produced and my role within it, I saw that God was absolutely first in every one; he was and is first with everything. It was clear that our preoccupancy with ourselves makes us blind to God's presence. I wondered how deep that perception held true, and to what level humility/abasement would assist us in our quest to acknowledge God and know our place with him. [63]

I examined the emotions, wants, and thoughts of my past that pushed me further away from what I had hoped

---

63   Abase: To make somebody feel belittled or degraded; *reflexive verb* to behave in a way that lowers your sense of dignity or self-esteem; however, I have given the word my own level of understanding.

to find. I thought about how many people today may feel pushback simply because they lack the ability to notice that their ego truly pulls one away from God. The wonderful perspective I now carry has complete reverence of God and I search for him in everything. I think of God in every moment. I came to acknowledge that he is the reason for everything, in everything, everywhere, always, and forever. I just could not see that until God showed me that to be close to him I would need to selflessly understand and continuously practice humility/abasement. I searched for the meaning of abasement, and the definition I found showed that it refers to a low or downcast state, depriving one of self-esteem. I thought that perhaps that definition was lacking insight when it came to being in abasement with God—it left too much open for interpretation to one who had thoughts of being close to God. I found that abasement/humility must be understood in order to be close to God and to see and understand what he does for us and gives to us everyday, beginning with the understanding that God is who he is.

As children of God, we cannot and should not try to label or judge God in any way—we do not have the ability. We must learn to see that we are whoever God says that we are, and for us to try to label ourselves as anything else would open the door for misinterpretation of one's own existence and one's place within it. We must understand that within our lives we cannot be anything other than who God allows us to be. In my experiences with God, I found that being in abasement with him felt as if to live in the fullness of who we were created to be, yet from a place of true humility in God's continuous presence. It's when we commit sin, and are centered on self or when we assume the role of anyone else (other than who we are) that we are pushed and pulled further away from closeness and conformity with God.

I then thought of others in my past who seemed to just be getting by in life, which prompted me to think about how I, too, was complacent in just about everything I had done. I tried hard to find examples of times I had lived without having myself first, but all I saw were moments of life in which I thought I was responsible for accomplishing many things. I could now see I thought more of me, myself, and I when I had wanted to do something. What I was blind to was that God was the one doing everything for me every day. God has always done that for everyone every day; that is how it has been since before the beginning of time, and it has been a lack of faith in God or lack of understanding of our place with God that has blinded us from truly seeing God. I found that even while we do the things we want to do, God is still there with us. There is no hiding from the truth, no hiding from the Father of all creation.

Now that I humbly live in abasement with God, he has shown me how to really live; God has now shown me the way. He allows me to awaken to a beautiful day each and every day; he helps me through every day and in everything, always; I have no want for anything; God accomplishes everything in my life (and in all of our lives) right on time, and he always has.

Prayer—the last resort

I've often prayed and seen others pray when things seem to be unmanageable in life, and I started wondering why it took so little, or so much, to unravel within a person's life before one became willing to pray and to ask God for help. I found those reasons to be one the most important parts of being in abasement with God. In studying the moments in my past when I prayed to God, and my motivations for doing so, I noticed that sometimes I prayed when I felt as if I had lost control. It was humbling and sometimes even mortifying events that helped in my understanding, and I was reminded that I cannot get through anything without God. It's in moments such as those that God will allow abasement/humility to occur.

I found some of the past decisions I made were causing pain, they were harmful to others and to me. It was while experiencing those challenging moments and thoughts that God began to teach me why it was we should be mindful of how we act and interact with everyone and with everything. Sometimes we don't understand why we cannot seem to get through a difficult time, God shows us the right way and that's a humbling or an abasing moment— humility happens sometimes when we feel as if we have no control over anything, he shows us we should have chosen perhaps more compassionately and considerately, and this helps us to move forward after learning how to properly act, and perceive our actions and decisions in the world.

When one hopes to get through whatever difficult moment one may be living through, God helps us by showing us that the way is within reach and this is with him and through humility and abasement. I found that while giving complete recognition and continual acknowledgement of God's endless greatness we may continue with him through each moment, this state of humility or abasement then allows us to continue moving forward in a perfect union with him. Abasement with God means that while being lowered in self-esteem, God then allows one's acts and confessions to bring forth feelings of humility. These selfless lessons can then be received while boldly and humbly moving forward with God.

Seek ultimate truth

God delights in our praises and glory; he loves the truthful and righteous to give him absolute recognition and continual acknowledgement. This allows each person who has reached a spiritually true, perfect and gentle union with him to become one with him. This is available to every person in search of the ultimate truth of love that is God. When God allows you to see his beauty and grace—what life is truly about—God shows you what you have been searching for your whole life. Living gracefully as one with him is living in abasement. By continuously having God first and foremost in everything and always, one gains a previously unnoticeable spiritual perspective, which is when true abasement with God transpires, and when we are truly allowed to see and to be close to him everyday. Surprisingly, I believed when I began the spiritual journey that I was in control of it. I had encountered a great many reasons that would indicate otherwise, yet God ultimately helped me see the greater truth—that it is God who has created each moment of life, not me and that as we perceive God as the father of all creation, understand his rightful place is always up above. *Thank-you, God.*

"And whoever exalts himself will be humbled, and he who humbles himself will be exalted" (MATTHEW 23:12)

Moving forward

When God first began to meet with me, our meetings would often transpire in very specific ways. At times I found it difficult to accept certain moments or move forward within them, which alarmed me; I could not understand why I could not get through something I thought I already understood. Later, God allowed me to recognize those moments as part of the beginning of my understanding of abasement. God was beginning to teach me, in a very unique way, how to be in his presence continuously. *Thank-you again, God.*

One faithful evening I had been learning and practicing all the different techniques I described earlier—meditating, focused breathing, fasting, praying, and centering my chakras in hopes of aligning my mind, body, and spirit with the moment; however, I was having difficulty within moving forward to the next moment. I realize now, thanks to God, that I was about to experience abasement—God allowed me to see that the difficulty I had been experiencing was not because of my technique, it was because both my personal behavior and my viewpoint were lacking truth. Each instance of the lowering of myself, either by God or by me, was created for me to fully understand the truth and consequences of my actions. I found one of the amazing truths of spirituality was that we are all capable of experiencing these graceful meetings with God . . . thanks to God. I began to see that my spiritual unions with God were occurring outside of what some say our normal five senses allow for, it was through the faithful belief that God is always with us and that with God anything is possible that I knew these meetings to be absolute truth. As I kept that mindset in perspective, and as my humbled meditative state reached a higher state of consciousness, I became even more focused on everything. God allowed me to see that my visual and audible perspective of God increased as each moment progressed.

Perhaps it was a combination of all the spiritual practices and techniques I had utilized prior to that moment that aided in that ability, but ultimately it is God who allowed it to be and allowed me to see. God was increasing in everything around me and I was decreasing in everything within every thought. It was with that humble and abasing perspective that I was truly able to understand that we all are always in the presence of God, everyday. If we will graciously acknowledge God's place as the father of all creation and the supreme Spirit of all things, and if we will learn to understand our places within his creation, we can all begin to be close to him. I found that this entire truth was possible because God allowed it and it happened because I was in abasement and conformity with him.

Humility in every moment

I began to apply my understanding of humility/abasement towards every internal and external moment, and I began to truly see what God was showing me. I could see that when my thoughts of God were of constant praise and of reverence of him, the moment continued revealing a wondrous sight of God and his glorious truth. When our next meeting began I was not sure what to expect or what would happen, but I knew that whatever it was, it would be great. At first, I could hear God's voice, he was speaking to me about my actions and about how I had been living, and then I began to see Jesus right next to me. Then God began to speak to me and show me how our spiritual meetings would truly begin.

A gentle and spiritual union began to form. I noticed the place we were in was something rather special—as I looked around I could see we were in a sitting area in the center of the room, and the room appeared to measure nearly two thousand square feet. Each wall was distinctive with faux patterns and styles adding to the rooms' brilliance. As the moment began, I had several loving thoughts of God that helped me to truly see him better. Then a thought came to mind that questioned my being there and I acted timid, I was immediately called out and was told to not act in such a way and a thought of self immediately took away from the moment, which had an opposite effect on the gentle union I was now forming with God. Instantly, God reversed that mindset inside of me, and once again I had another abasing thought of God and of how wonderful and great he is. The gentle spiritual union with God grew in magnitude as we moved forward in our conversation. I continued to see Jesus sitting right next to me, and while he continued to teach me how our spiritual union formed, he then began to reveal that when great minds come together in humility and abasement, the ability to form these gentle and spiritual unions with him become possible.

God, you always reveal unimaginable
greatness. You are magnificent and beautiful
in every way. Your presence is breathtaking;
you are who you are; you are God.

What an entrance

Then as the music played in the background Jesus pointed to one particular location within the room I needed to pay close attention to. The entire spiritual meeting initially began with the perspective of what flash video or shutter vision appears like; I noted that was how all our spiritual unions would begin. I could see something occurring in an area several feet wide and several feet across, about fifteen feet away from us. Something was bubbling up and it overflowed in similar way to how water or even molten magma does; however, it was reminiscent of something that was both a solid and a liquid. I blinked several times and adjusted the position of my head in my effort to figure out what it was, and something distinctive began to rise up through the thick substance. I looked to Jesus, hoping he would explain what I was witnessing, but he again motioned to look at what was happening before us. Suddenly God our fathers supreme Spirit arose from the bubbling area. He then shook his whole body, and the substance he had just risen through began to fall off of him . . . and there he hovered. It was in that moment that God helped me to see what truly became possible when humble/abased minds are in a spiritual union with him. God, our father; Jesus, our Lord; and I had just been joined in a gentle and loving spiritual union. In that place there are wondrous sights to behold, and in that place it's possible for us to always be close to him and to see him spiritually. *What an entrance,* I thought.

Then God our father began to rise up and glide and fly around the room. He flew around us while Jesus and I sat and I could see He was dressed in clothes reminiscent of what people of early civilizations wore thousands of years ago, again something resembling a praetorian, I noted his body armor. I have never seen such grace and style as I observed in God's movements in, around, and through that place—around that corner and around another entrance way, gliding up and around a bend, and then out of the room with his arm stretched outwardly and his legs positioned perfectly as he soared up. I looked at Jesus and saw that he was still observing God our father, who was still visible although he was not within the viewing area of the room we were in; he was still visibly soaring through the walls. In another instant he flew upward and out of the whole area and then came back down and suddenly was again in the room, sitting across from Jesus and me. Abasement, and its subsequent gentle and spiritual union with God, shows us what we have truly been seeking all of our lives—God and his incredible beauty.

Another spiritual meeting

There we sat—God, our father; Jesus, our Lord and Savior; the Holy Spirit, and I—talking about how wonderful everything is with them. We began speaking of the delivery of the book, which had already been written but needed some editing. God, our father began explaining to me that I needed to edit specific chapters and was pointing out that specific lines and certain words needed to be changed. I paid close attention to him and I didn't realize that there was much that still needed to be edited and changed. Then God did something wonderful, he showed me the artist (who was singing and playing on the radio) who then began performing spiritually in our presence. It was Elvis Costello, and he was dancing and singing "Every day I write the book" in the background. My past momentary glimpses of transcendence with music, literature, and film became even clearer as God allowed me to witness its capabilities, and I was repeatedly aware that I was seeing more clearly because of God and our spiritual union. I have always enjoyed listening to music—I often play it throughout the day, and music was playing in my room before that particular spiritual union had begun; however, God was now showing me what being in a spiritual union with him and listening to music would truly allow for.

I noticed the artist on the radio station was still spiritually in attendance, and while God was allowing me to pay careful attention to our conversation, I began to notice each subsequent artist sing and dance around us. Then God stopped speaking for a while and we all began to observe the artists performing their songs: Coldplay, then Adele, and then several others. Each artist playing, singing, and in attendance was singing a message that was directly in alignment with our conversations and Gods expressed points to me. God had revealed that my previous insight into transcendence and the arts was truly a small part of what God spiritually allows for—when we are fully in a gentle spiritual union and humility/abasement with God, we are not just connecting with the artist and experiencing a form of transcendence. If we pay careful attention to the moment, our lives, the music, and our surroundings, we will find God is always speaking to us. That happened with each new song that played and with each new artist, and each song sung and performed fit the moment perfectly. God utilized specific lyrics to get his message across, as he has always done so with me. I truly love the way God communicates, it's so incredible. *Thank-you, God, for sharing that spiritually insightful moment.*

God searched my heart and saw that I was in need of another lesson. Instantly a person who I had been fond of was spiritually there. God then explained to me that the feelings I had for this person needed to be addressed. I spoke to this person about how I now considered my past behavior to be inappropriate, and I asked for forgiveness. I had lied to this person about several things and it was here in this meeting that I asked to be forgiven for my untruthful remarks. I was forgiven and then we all began to speak and enjoy the company of God for a while longer. I knew God was helping me to obtain peace from that experience and showing me how I was truly in need of abasement and offered me redemption. He was beginning to teach me abasement and humility.

Certainty

As we moved further past that spiritual observation and into the next moment, God showed me certainty in everything—knowing that everything is of him. God showed me what it means to be fearless of everything with him. God showed me how to love everything with him. God helped me to realize that in my spiritual union with him, it's always so wonderful to say to him, "You are great, God, and thank-you for showing me the way." God spoke with me for a great while longer about the tasks I needed to accomplish. As the conversation continued through the night, God added what I needed to edit to my memory. I knew that I had much work to do and that this journey was still revealing many spiritual insights and truths. I went to sleep shortly thereafter and upon awakening, I realized that yet again, my perspective of everything within life had changed.

I could see that each spiritual union and meeting is as different and unique as the next. That recent one made me see that I simply am a part of the greatness of life. Despite all that I was lacking—my lack of understanding of myself and my place with God—life is life and it is always great with God. I know now that some of my past behavior required abasement by God to fully understand the truth of my actions and to allow comprehension of my unity with God. God brought forth each moment of humility by showing me that I had many emotions and thoughts of control, doubt, uncertainty, anger, resentment, and ego. He taught me that those thoughts and emotions were lacking in every way, and that I needed to experience them in a way that could allow each lesson to truly be felt, understood, and then learned. I did find that within each lesson, God would allow for the moment of redemption but it was only after the lesson of abasement was truly understood and acknowledged. That was how I began to understand humility and complete abasement with God.

Reduction

An incredible part of learning of humility/abasement with God is the understanding of what it truly means to be reduced and to consider oneself as nothing. For me, that meant to let go of everything I thought I once held onto and to become lower than I thought was once possible. God revealed his truth after each lesson I survived in his special and abasing way, whether it was a lesson in humility, mortification, dishonor, degradation, disgrace, or any other abasing way God saw fit to teach me. It was exactly what I needed in order to learn of such truth as only God can teach.

To go through such abasing moments truthfully, one must be willing to accept everything and want for nothing— God showed me the way out of a difficult moment was to accept it, endure it, and to trust in him. I was to trust that each moment was created specifically for me, and that in order to move forward and toward him, I had to recognize each lesson and totally accept it while giving thanks and praise to God for having it. God also showed me that if I had difficulty understanding a lesson, he would continue to remind me and continue to show me over again, and in an unimaginable way, until I did understand.

As God allowed me to humbly reach each point of understanding, I wondered how I could possibly assist those also in search of such wondrous moments with God. I began searching for the constants within that led to this moment, I realized:

- I thought of God constantly with each and every thought.
- I sought God constantly with each and every breath.
- I constantly paid careful attention to each moment of God's creation.

- I constantly hoped to better understand what God's plan is for me and for all of us.
- With each recognition and acknowledgement of God's magnificence, a perfect gentle and spiritual union with him is possible.

Devotion

The word "devout" means devoted to divine worship *or* to express devotion or earnest sincerity. God showed me that by applying earnest sincerity and devotion towards my understandings of humility/abasement with him, he would reveal how each spiritual union forms.

He clearly showed me that truth one evening while I was in search of him—focused, continuously thinking of him, considering him with each emotion, and earnestly in need of seeing him. I thought that it should not be difficult to find and to be close to him because he is everywhere, always and forever. As I focused on God, he began to reveal that I was further in need of humility and abasement. He showed me that even though I thought of and sought him earnestly, my heart was lacking the proper emotional and thoughtful considerations one must have in order to be close to him. I was in need of a big lesson. God searched my heart again and found that I was lacking in many ways. He could see everything within. He could see all that I had covered up or looked over or looked away from in my life. He knew instantly what I needed and began to teach me in the most unimaginable ways. *Bless you and thank-you, God; you are all knowing.*

God began by first showing me that I needed to understand my thoughts, emotions, and actions better, and that I was in greater need of humility. He explained that I had done many things in my life selfishly and inconsiderately, and that I was still behaving that way. God is always right and always tells the truth, and as I thought of what he told me, I was instantly covered in shame. I acknowledged him and said,

"God, you're right. I have done these things and I am sorry. Will you please forgive me?" I was feeling low at that point, and I began to wonder how I could have done the things God spoke of when the next abasing lesson began—one to bring me even lower than before.

He pointed out to me that I had committed wrongful acts that dishonored me and everyone else I had ever mistreated or harmed. God was showing me that I needed to reconsider, understand, and recognize the wrong in each of those acts in order to be close to him. I felt mortified and disgraced, and I began to cry and feel the presence of something I did not understand—a feeling God called penitence—a gift that humbled me to nothing in order to be close to him. I had never felt as low as I did before that moment; I felt crushed, and so far removed from whom I thought I was. It was hurting so bad to know that I had done so many things in life in that manner, but God was helping me to reach an understanding of who I am, where I am, and why I am by allowing me to better understand my place with him. It was in that downcast state when God then lifted me up and said,

"Okay, Now I can look at you." He was helping me to realize what I was in need of before he exalted me, and allowed us to move forward together.

Feel his presence

God then showed me that one amazing aspect of being in spiritual union with him was being able to feel his presence and to truly feel him speaking inside me. God revealed also that when he requires my undivided attention, he has special ways of letting me know—ways that are completely noticeable when I pay close attention. God's unique ways of getting my attention while in conformity all differ: At times it feels like a short and quick tap on my body (which, by the way, is in a different location every time he needs me to notice something specific), accompanied by his soft whisper; at other times he allows me to notice something only he and I know about. I also know when it's God because my body begins to quiver and tremble in his presence. I later learned that this is what is meant by trembling before the lord.

Doubt or uncertainty

God allowed me to realize that gentle and kind considerations, praise, and grace towards him all helped our spiritual union to flourish by leaps and bounds. Complete recognition and the continual acknowledgement of his endless greatness allows for endless possibilities.

As that gentle and spiritual union formed and we continued forward with my next observation, I could see a red light and a set of five steps directly before me rising upward. I began to earnestly focus on traversing each step when, suddenly, I began to slowly move in an upward direction towards the top of the stairs. I felt the movement like I was in an out-of-body state. I could clearly see I was in another area very similar to the one I had been in previously with God and Jesus, but as I began to move up the stairs, I had a fearful thought that was caused by doubt and uncertainty of the unknown—I could feel myself slipping away from the spiritual union I had just formed with God. I tried to shake off the thought, adjust my mindset, and continue forward. God then allowed me to regain focus, and once again I began to move upward and over the stairs.

I was now on another level and moving through a hallway towards an opening on the other end, nearly forty feet away. The hallway had opened sections to the left similar to closets and when I reached the end of the hall, the path turned to the left and a grand area opened up. I noticed three angels standing at the end of the hall just as I turned the corner of the hallway and stepped into the larger area. I then saw five large boulders, twelve feet tall and ten feet wide, spaced twenty feet from one another and then stretched from wall to wall. Several more rows of rocks off-set each other behind the ones in front. The large area had no visible ceiling, and when I looked to the back of it, I could see that it continued for another hundred yards past the boulders before bending again towards the left. The walls were spaced about a hundred-and-twenty yards from each other. Suddenly another fearful thought grabbed hold of me and instilled in me enough doubt to stop me from earnestly staying focused on God and our union. Our union ceased instantly, and I was back where I had started.

When we stay earnestly focused on God with good, true, pure, and loving thoughts, there are incredible sights to behold and there is nothing ever to fear.

A divine lesson

I then talked with God about what was happening and thankfully felt completely peaceful again. Once again, I noticed I was before God, our father, Jesus, our lord, and The Holy Spirit, each member of the Trinity was completely visible right next to me. A spiritual union had formed once more with them, and I felt complete and serene. I moved my right arm, and just as I touched the wall next to me, I felt the presence of God. I looked at where my hand met the wall and saw God was touching one small part of my hand! I smiled, and in the blink of an eye my surroundings had changed yet again. In the same moment, God allowed me to see him entering our spiritual union: I could see the entire perspective begin with what stop/start shutter vision would look like. The spiritual union we had just formed for some reason had a darker, reddish color which was considerably different to my view of previous unions with God. God helped me to see that my heart and my point of view towards the moment was in need of some careful consideration. When my emotions and thoughts changed to a more reverential and devoted perspective, one with more humility, selflessness, and considerate thoughts of him, the darker and reddish colors instantly changed to a lighter bluish-white color. Then as soon as I observed that, and my perspectives changed God fully entered into our spiritual union.

To my right, hovering horizontally several feet above what I could see of the ground, I recognized God's supreme spirit entering the moment as only God does, wonderfully and uniquely God. God our father then began to once more fly all around the area in his spectacular way. His free-flowing form once again appeared to move through the walls, and as he did, his form was just as visible as if he were still completely within the immediate area. The area we were now in resembled an outdoor amphitheater, only the amphitheater was situated slightly above me. I had to look upward at a thirty-degree angle to get a direct view of it, and then we began to move forward while we spoke of what this lesson would reveal. As the walls on each side of us rose upwardly, and again I could not see a ceiling as we slowly moved—turning gradually from side to side, making forward progress—God continued to speak with me of humility/abasement and of my understanding of how to speak to him. God was showing me someplace incredible, it was a place unlike anything I had ever seen before.

While we spoke in this incredible location that resembled an outdoor amphitheater I knew God, our father, Jesus, our lord and the Holy Spirit and I, were directly before many other brilliant and unique beings within this place. I understood some of them to be deity and some of them to be angels. I could see many of them positioned up the slopes on the left and on the right, and as the lessons continued the Holy Spirit began to show me something rather extraordinary. In an instant we transcended to another place altogether. I didn't quite understand at the time that I had conformed to be one with the lord and that in an instant we had moved somewhere else. As the Holy Spirit and I were moving through this lesson to reveal what I had been called there to see, she moved slightly ahead of me and as I continued to follow her I flew and then seemed to pass straight through her. I was not sure as to what this lesson was revealing or even how to respond to the experience. We began to talk about it, and suddenly I found myself having challenging lessons being shown to me as our conversation revolved around how wonderful the experience truly was. I still found it difficult to remain focused even with all the amazing experiences happening all around me.

Words of abasement

I thought I knew how to be close to God. I found that I kept stumbling and couldn't quite get the conversations straight; I seemed to still be missing the lesson. I would often speak quickly, without proper consideration, and God our father was instructing me on how to speak to him in an abasing and humble way. I expressed to God that I thought I was. Suddenly I felt someone place his finger over my mouth, but it was God shushing me, and incredibly he was using the edge of the blanket to do this. He then told me he was going to count every abasing way that I spoke to him, and that for every form of abasement, he would add one second to the incredible thing he was about to show to me. He told me I would have thirty seconds to say as many abasing things to him as I could and I thought *Okay, I can do that.* At first I gave praise and thanks to God for each lesson he had shown me, and for each experience I had been a part of. I thanked him for many wonderful things when I realized he hadn't even begun counting yet. I had to carefully reconsider my perspective. I felt the power of the lesson and I said something abasing and humbling to God our father, and I heard Jesus say,

"That's one."

Then I praised and thanked him again, but he did not count that as abasement. I was feeling awkward but starting to see the lesson: I had been praising and giving thanks to God, but I had not had the proper abasing perspective needed to remain close to him. I spoke to God in another abasing way again. Then Jesus counted, saying,

"That's two,"

As I continued and said something else in abasement, Jesus continued counting. That continued for thirty seconds, and I managed to speak to God in sixteen abasing ways in that time. Then God said,

"Okay, here we go!"

The end of a place

In another instant we transcended to a beautiful world that was filled with vibrant landscapes and regal mountains and other living things I had not ever seen before. I saw immense rocky plains filled with undergrowth and patchy grass; I saw rolling emerald hills and a matchless vitality in those living there, and clearly I could see they were moving about in an unusual way. God began to explain to me how important true spiritual unions and abasement with him are and how the world we are in lacked it. He showed me people's poor spiritual unions and perspectives and how their lack of abasement would make their world come to an end.

We moved past several unique rocks whose formations and mobility indicated they were actually alive with vitality. These extraordinary rocks were simply three moving rows of rock several feet long and were separated by a foot. The two outer rows moved in unison, and the inner row moved in the opposite direction. Next we moved past a rocking chair rocking back and forth with the vitality of a figure sitting upon it; I noticed it had a little red glowing light. We moved from there and came across four more of the little red glowing lights along the vast rocky stretch of land and then we came upon a green valley. I could see God was ending that place.

As this incredible event began I didn't know how to act or how to respond. I observed the fear and panic of all those who lived there; I could see them running to the ends of the world, clearly this event was happening to their entire world and I felt sad for them, but I couldn't cry. I expressed how I felt about that moment.

I said, *oh my God, oh my goodness.* God saw that my words and my behavior were lacking conviction and truth and began to further explain my behavior to me and what I was looking at as he then called me out. God was showing me the truth of abasement in a very unique way. Then I saw a mountain suddenly get up and walk away; I saw every rock before us get up and then step into one of many giant holes that were placed in the center of some open areas upon the otherworld's surface, and instantly they vanished into oblivion. I saw large sections of that world rolling into themselves while the many people who lived there stared in amazement at what was happening all around them. I saw many forms of life all ending as their time there was terminated. I saw a man and woman standing atop of what looked like the drum tower of a castle, which sat directly along the side of a mountain cliff. They were dressed formally and wearing nice clothing and I could see they had something protruding from them that resembled wings on their backs.

I expressed out loud again to God how devastating it all was and how I felt about it, and I didn't realize those nearby would hear me expressing my thoughts. Suddenly one of the persons on the edge of this great mountain saw us and began speaking directly to God. I could hear the fear in his voice, I could hear him asking God to save him and help him. Then he jumped from the edge of a cliff. The mountain then turned into itself and ended. The being who had jumped grabbed hold of us and I could literally feel him holding onto me firmly. I didn't know what to say to him as he pleaded to God, so there he hung for several more moments. I heard the person asking if it was okay to stay with us. I didn't know how to respond. God asked me what I was going to do about this person. I then told that person who had jumped to us, he could stay as long as God allowed it. Then as that world continued to close in on itself and end, I began to see many spirits of those from that world rising up towards heaven. I could hear the voice of the person who had grabbed hold of me and who was now moving with us along our journey. We traveled for a little while longer observing.

We then moved back to where we had begun, back to where our spiritual meeting and union before the lesson and observation had occurred. I spoke with God for a while longer about what had just happened and all that I had witnessed. I could see that the person who had joined us, like the many of the spirits before him began to then rise up toward heaven. We began to once more move about an amazing spiritual realm and I began to notice other incredible places, one after another. I could see we made our way back to the place where the outdoor amphitheater was. We stayed joined as one and in conversation while we spoke about the wondrous experiences of his creations. As the meeting came closer to an end it was clear that we had made what seemed like a full circle and God revealed a little red light and a set of five steps directly before me which rose upward and seemed very familiar, and God then helped me to understand that we were back where we had first begun. Back where the five steps lead upward to a hallway and once again I was completely amazed with God.

Abasing thoughts

To think of God and to be close to God is truly wonderful and beautiful. He has shown me the way and with him I am complete. I found the importance of that lesson to be that our spiritual unions can form in many ways, and to have a spiritual union with God, we must continuously learn how to apply earnest sincerity and devotion to him. It was here with good, true, pure, and loving thoughts that our spiritual union knew no bounds, that we joined to be one and that all things are truly possible.

God, I thank you for the incredible journey.

When those humbling moments and abasing conversations I've had with God come to mind, I can remember them beginning something like this:

God, your love is everlasting. God, you are great. Thank-you for all you have ever done. You created every moment and you have created each one perfect. You are everywhere in everything and you are all knowing. You are good and true with all that you do. You give purpose and meaning to each life you have created. You give inspiration its inspiration and are perfect in every way. You give us all hope with each breath. God, without you there is no me. God, you are wonderful. Thank-you, thank-you, and thank-you for showing us the way every day. God, the peacefulness of each moment's beauty, the sound of everything in perfect harmony, the sight of a joyful existence, and the hope of life's understanding all come from you, and I thank you for your love. With your love I can achieve all that you allow me to, and I bless you and praise you with each breath you give to me. Each day is exactly the way you allow it to be—perfect, true, and complete with you. The wind blows in the direction you say and like the wind, I, too, shall listen for you and to you with every breeze. I love you, God; you are incredible, amazing; and your happiness is great. Your love is the best; with you, I know I can do anything. I love everything that is good and true, and I know it's because of you. Thank-you for each breath I take and thank you for each lesson in life. I can, I will, and I do because of you. Thank-you, God, for another day of hope; and thank-you, God, for another day of love. Everything is always great with you and I thank you for showing me the way today and every day. God,

237

you are excellence in all that you do, and all that
you do is excellent. God, I love you and bless you. I
thank you for the sound of thunder that happens the
moment you ask it to; I thank you for each raindrop
that falls when you allow it; I thank you for the
wind that blows the instant that you tell it to, and I
thank you for each breath you give to us all. God,
the beauty of your world is amazing, and I thank
you for each and every sight you allow me to see.
You are great in all that you do; it is you
in all that I see. I thank you and I love
you with the love you give to me.
Thank-you, God.

Above, Below, and Beyond

All thanks to God and thanks to being in abasement with God, I could feel the emotional warmth God had shared with me while teaching me how to be close to him. I thought of the narrowest path again and what it truly means to walk upright. God had shown me how to live with honor and moral, and I knew of the unbearable consequences of not abiding by the word of God. My heart filled with sorrow for those who could not find their way, or those who had chosen a path with self centered ego, or self-destruction rather than a path of having God first and loving all of his creation. When I thought about those who walked about the world with their eyes closed, I realized I, too, had once walked in the same way. I now wondered if they even cared, and then I found myself hoping and praying for those who seemed to go through life unaware of the blindness to their self-serving and self-consuming lives they seemed to be living. Knowing now that such paths lead away from God, and then learning that while being in abasement and sharing a spiritual union with him allows his presence to become totally recognizable in every life, I could see everything is possible for those who learn to open their eyes and hearts to the truth.

The careful observance of God's astounding synchronicity helps open the door to spirituality and contributes directly to a better understanding, to knowledge, and also to wisdom. From newborn babe to maturity, each of has the responsibility to learn as we grow and develop in this magical world. I liken my experiences to having been born again spiritually—each insightful and spiritual revelation resembling the early lessons of childhood. The observance of prescience and of the energy we all have within is comparable to learning to walk or talk spiritually; the observance of the occurrence of the supernatural and of enlightenment seems comparable to both running and/or flying; each wonderful moment leading to the next to build the spiritual unions and foundations I needed in order to reach an understanding of what it truly means to be in a gentle spiritual conformity with God.

A powerful lesson

For several days before these meetings began I had been fasting, praying, and meditating continuously in search of God with what seemed like each breath. I often thought of our previous meetings and spiritual unions of conformity, and as I earnestly moved forward in seeking a spiritual union with him, I hoped and prayed that our next meeting would be soon. I had been intensely focused and yearning to fully understand each of the lessons God continued to teach me. I could feel his presence everywhere and then, thankfully, God allowed our spiritual meeting to once more begin.

Our meetings had the miraculous power of God completely within them. I could sense God all around me and in everything, everywhere, and always, and then God began to teach me another lesson in abasement before I could truly conform and be in his presence. God, Jesus, the Holy Spirit, and I began conversing on truthfulness, sincerity, love, and life. God began by showing me I was lacking in all of them, starting with the truth. God explained while I listened. He had searched my heart and he knew of each untruthful word, thought, and emotion I had ever felt, thought of doing, or felt like speaking. He showed me each instance when I had selfishly withheld, manipulated, or attempted to control the truth. The realization of the severity of my past actions mortified me. God was showing me many circumstances I had not been truthful, loving, and kind in. I began to cry, and as the tears began to roll down my cheeks, I heard God's wonderful voice explaining how I had so carelessly affected lives and loves. God spoke truthfully of the many relationships I had entered into insincerely, speaking directly of specific moments and instances of pain, sorrow, and grief I had directly been a part of or caused. With the tears streaming from my eyes, I found it difficult to hear the truth of my actions. I had not truly lived the gentle, good, and loving life I thought I did, or that I had hoped to.

I felt humiliated, low, and ashamed of my actions. I confessed to all God showed me, and I began to truly understand that I was now in the father and the father was in me once again as he exalted me and lifted me up. I was to learn now of what it truly meant to live as one with him. God taught me that if I had any difficulty understanding any moment of life, any moment at all, that all I needed to do was humbly ask him to help me and he would. He would ask me to ask Jesus, I would then ask Jesus, and then Jesus would reveal the way. God would then allow us to move forward in spiritual union. I was truly thankful for God showing me how to truly live as one with him and what our unions would allow for. The grandeur of grace and excellence from God is remarkable and glorious, and to live in such a perfect and divine manner is truly wonderful to witness and to be a part of.

God's perfect spiritual union is unlike any other union, spiritual or otherwise. Its inception, conformation, formation, realization, confirmation, and extent are unfathomable. Thanks to God, I have seen a great many spiritual unions form. I have also seen how different people's formations can be if those in spiritual union, lack abasement, and are self-serving or self-consuming. While they conform visually in a similar manner to one another, their formations are very different to those I witness in a selfless, gentle, spiritual union with him. Surprisingly, those lacking abasement and spiritual conformity with God all appeared to form in the same way. I could see their unions forming with one another but they all lacked the emotional and thoughtful perspectives of God which allow for each limitless union with him to grow without bounds. God was teaching me that when one is in union with him only then can one truly see what it means to live as one with him and to truly be spiritually great.

"But he who is joined to the Lord is one spirit with Him" (1 CORINTHIANS 6:17)

Receiving the Holy Spirit

To visibly see and be in the immediate presence of God, our father; Jesus Christ, our Lord; and the Holy Spirit is beyond words—it's absolutely supreme. As I thought of how incredible it was to be meeting with them again, God graced me with an immediate smile. As our union grew in magnitude, our standing positions slowly became more relaxed. Before long we were sitting, standing, moving about, talking, sharing, and enjoying each other's company, just as with the closest of friendships developed over a lifetime. A spiritual union with divinity reveals God's omnipotence when, and only when, God allows for such a revelation to be seen.

God asked me to receive the Holy Spirit and instructed me to breathe in deeply. I did so several times. Each inhalation was filled with love and grace. As I exhaled, I could feel a tingling sensation throughout my entire body; and when I looked in the direction of my breath, I saw many small and circular particles of energy coming from my mouth and rising upwardly above me. When I put my hands together in prayer, I could see the same bright light emanating from my folded hands. I could see the power of prayer rising upward toward God. The sensational feelings of the Holy Spirit within grew with each breath, and I understood the trembling sensation I was once again experiencing what it means to tremble before the Lord. I had not quite yet made the connection between being in God's presence and my body trembling until that very moment. God and I began to speak specifically about how the trembling is one way he indicates to us all that we are in his direct presence. As the moment progressed and we moved forward, I felt completely revived, refreshed, and full of vigor.

Before long I noticed our spiritual union growing as I got better at placing God in his rightful place above me and realized I had conformed to be as one with the Lord. God would speak of how wonderful a moment was and I would speak of how wonderful God was in the moment, how wonderful God allowed me to feel in the moment, and how the moment felt wonderful because God allowed me to feel it. Conversations like that continued for hours, with God revealing truths with each thought I had about anything good and true.

The gates of heaven

I had learned that to be near God I would need to be in abasement with God, and that for me to remain close to him I would continue to need to conform to him in abasement.

Then I felt someone grab hold of my right arm just around my bicep. I looked and saw an angel—I believe it was the archangel Gabriel; then I felt the sensation of another grabbing hold of me on the left arm, and then I was lifted up directly before God. We hovered there for several moments before God gave a command. A tiny black hole then became visible and increased in size until it became fully dilated to become a temporal portal into another realm. Light particles around the place where the circumference of the doorway opened seemed to fall into that place, and then incredibly we entered.

As the angel held me tight, we flew upward between two worlds for several minutes. We traveled at such an incredible speed that my arms and legs dangled behind, and when I looked back at the angel, I saw his great wings at work. We then came upon the cornerstone of an enormous structure whose great walls continued in a ninety-degree direction. We had flown with great speed and agility, as high as the first section; but there were many more levels above us, each constructed with precise angles and perfect measurements. The walls were brilliant and appeared to be made of brilliant stone. The whole edifice was radiating brightly, and it had a soft beige pearly color. The angel flew me upward, and then around and through several other sections that all seemed to be part of an entrance. Then we flew over an enormous gate and great wall that stretched in both directions and then faded away into the vastness—the gates of heaven.

We then flew towards a mountain range and began to fly over their sheer cliffs and crevasses. The angel held onto me tightly and flew us in closer until I could see movement along the rocky surface—a formation of rocks moving in a very distinct way—the same type of rock formations I had seen earlier with God during another lesson in abasement. The vitality of those rock formations was showing me that even the rocks are alive in heaven. We flew forward and approached another wondrous sight. I saw endless rocks falling over the edge of a cliff and tumbling down a slope to gather at its base. Some rocks were extremely large while others were small in size—but each one was distinctive. I could hear their sounds as they tumbled down the slopes, crushing into one another and then coming to a stop. They were reminiscent of a waterfall made entirely of rocks. We flew in closer to one of the mountains and I could see other people just like those who I had seen rising up toward heaven in a previous lesson of abasement with God. Every place in this incredible kingdom was absolutely beautiful.

We then left that place and traveled great distances with each breath, periodically passing many unique places and those that lived in those parts of heaven. As we came closer to them, I heard them asking us about the nature of our visit and as the angel Gabriel conveyed to them what we were doing there, I heard them speaking in greater depths of our journey and then we'd fly off again. We then approached several other very unique and distinct beings in a similar way. We left from there toward an incredible sight of mountains and I could now see that the angel's flight appeared to be in unison with my emotional state of abasement with God. Then suddenly while in flight, I had one instance of fear arise from somewhere within; I was not sure what it was about, and it could only be described as a panic attack. I think it could have been because all my thoughts of the journey turned to questions about how was it that I was there, and I began to have doubts. Before I knew it, I saw what I believed to be another angel falling from us towards the ground. I wasn't sure what had just happened, but I saw firsthand that doubt is not allowed in heaven. Thankfully, we kept flying. Once more we covered vast areas, seemingly with each inhalation and exhalation I took. Next we came upon another large mountain, where the views of a valley below and many of those living there also came into view. I could see the different shades of white, tan, and fiery red in the stone that formed the mountains. I would later learn these were the same mountains spoken of in The Book of Revelation by Jesus Christ. Then I saw a man standing along the fiery red mountains and as we approached him I spoke aloud saying how amazing this was. Then I noticed the ground shook and the man lost his footing and tumbled down one of the slopes along the mountain side. I wasn't sure how this had happened but we continued flying from there. As I looked to the right of those mountains I saw green grass on the endless rolling hills below and incredible scenery in every direction.

An angelic wall

From that place we flew upward yet again and then entered into another portal which led us above this level of heaven into the beyond yonder—and into somewhere and nowhere once more—and then we started to fly directly toward some event happening before us. I noticed it was a large assembly of angels coming together. They stretched themselves out in a vertical and horizontal way; they then began to form a type of wall which extended upward and outward into the great abyss we were flying though, and I noticed they too seem to fade away into the abyss. Each angel stretched itself out like an X, with his hands grabbing hold of the angel above him and with his feet grabbed onto by the angel beneath him. I could see their feet were just like their hands. The angels all linked together as we approached them, possibly creating the barrier to keep out those who were not allowed to enter the area beyond that point. As we flew downward slightly and came within a few feet of them all, I could see them in great detail. They looked just like many other angels I had seen in the past years, they had distinct angel faces with angel eyes, no hair, and a slightly elongated face. Then I heard a voice say,

"What are you doing here?"

Then the angel who held onto me said, "God has allowed him to be here."

Then one angel stepped aside and allowed me passage. I could see the wood floors and bright vivid colors of yet another level of heaven. Just as I was about to step in, I thought about God and how I had hoped to be close to him again, so I decided to return back to God and asked the angel who was holding onto me if I could.

We suddenly left the area with the assembly of angels in that abyss, and once again we were flying high above the previous level of heaven. We flew over the hills and valleys and I could see the mountain ranges extending into the distance. At one point we came upon a large group of people moving about, and we hovered hundreds of feet above them all. We stayed only for a moment and then flew in the direction of the fiery mountains again. We came in closer. I could see that same person standing there on the mountains, gazing downwards towards the valley, and as we came right up to him and observed him more closely. I could hear him speaking to me, his voice was faint and sounded tiny, and I knew he was speaking about what had happened earlier. I was thankful he was okay, then I listened to what he said for a moment and then we moved on. Again we flew passing all the previous locations from before, rising and descending with inhales and exhales of breath, past the highest peaks, past the cliffs and crevasses, past the rockfalls and the moving rock formations, and along the jagged mountain slopes until we reached the magnificent mountain peaks we first flew by. Up and over the pearly gated entrance of heaven, we continued to fly downward with superlative agility and great speed of descent. Down, down we sped navigating the same levels of the entrance until we reached another temporal portal. It was again in the shape of a large sphere, and once we had entered into it, the journey was nearly instant. We were again in the direct presence of the Holy Trinity, back where we started our journey.

A dark pit

God asked me about my journey, how I felt, and why I chose to return at the moment I did. I replied,

"I wasn't ready to enter into the place behind that assembly of angels just yet, and I wanted to be near you again."

He asked me about the meeting with the person on the mountain and I said, "I didn't realize my voice would have that sort of affect on the place."

I was trying to make better sense of the whole experience. Then I asked God, "What about that other place?"

Instantly God knew which place I was talking about. Shortly after I asked that question, I felt the same angel grabbing hold of my arms and lifting me up once more, and once again we hovered before God until, at his command, another temporal portal began to open. A tiny black hole appeared before us and began to dilate to a size large enough for us to fly through. The entrance was different than before, though, and was pitch black. Once it became large enough for us to move through, God allowed us to pass. As we did so, I saw a large black figure move across the entrance in front of us. I saw a long tail that trailed the dark being and then rolled over itself (like a snake's tail) as it reached the other side of the entrance. The being turned and stared at us as we flew by, and I could see his glowing eyes and the outline of his horns and I knew who it was. We kept on moving forward; I could see darkness everywhere, and black smoke billowing up in many places. The walls were covered in black soot and had many interconnecting passages and every room had a slight grey color on their walls. I could feel the presence of those suffering nearby, the absence of light, and the pain, misery, and torments of all those who were lost and stuck in such a loveless place. It was a lightless, dark, cold, and unsavory dwelling.

God had allowed a wonderful view of heaven and now he was showing me insights and unique views into hell, but I didn't want to be there anymore, and I realized there was no visible exit. Instantly I began to pray to God, our Father, and focus all my thoughts onto him. I prayed the Lord's Prayer:

> *"Our Father who art in heaven,*
> *hallowed be thy name.*
> *Thy kingdom come.*
> *Thy will be done*

on earth as it is in heaven.
Give us this day our daily bread,
and forgive us our trespasses,
as we forgive those who trespass against us,
and lead us not into temptation,
but deliver us from evil.
For thine is the kingdom,
and the power, and the glory,
for ever and ever.

Amen."

I could feel God's grace while I prayed, and when I had concluded the Lord's Prayer, I began to think of all the abasing lessons and moments God had shared with me. With each thought I continued to give thanks and praise to God for all he does—for giving, for loving, for sharing, for caring, for providing us with everything—as he has always done since before the beginning. Amazingly, God began lifting us up, foot by foot, with each extoller. I continued focusing onto God by saying,

"Bless you, God, you are great."

"God you are amazing."

"Thank-you, God, for all you do."

"Thank-you for such a wonderful journey."

I prayed to God continuously and humbly, giving earnest thoughts and thanks to him as he gradually allowed us to ascend from the dark pit. I could see first hand how our prayers and thankfulness to God directly help us all move closer to him. The walls gradually began to regain color—they changed slowly from black and grey to light brown, and then to lighter colors altogether. As the visible characteristics of that dark and desolate place faded, God allowed an opening up above us for us to move through. The opening which became visible once we had flown upward for hundreds of feet was circular, and just the opposite of our entry into the dark pit. The exit was shaped like a long cylindrical tunnel that rose straight up, and the angel flew us through it until we were once again in the direct presence of God.

Bridling thoughts

I felt many emotions with having just witnessed such a place, and while I cannot understand why I would purposefully think the thought I had next, I had a brief thought that allowed for one instance of uncertainty to creep in. Perhaps it was another way God was teaching me to comprehend such a lesson, or perhaps it was a choice that I had made without understanding the consequences; I did not ask, but I had not been able to bridle my thoughts. My abased perspective of my experience shifted, and once again I was instantly in that dark pit. God showed me in one instant that those who do not, have not, or will not keep God first are destined to vanish from him. I was instantly away from God and away from the union that we had shared while I had conformed to him in abasement.

> *"But the wicked will perish; And the enemies of the Lord, like the splendor of the meadows, shall vanish. Into smoke they shall vanish away."* (PSALM37:20).

Thankfully, God allowed me to put my hands together and recite the Lord's Prayer once again, giving thanks and praise to him. I focused all thoughts on the grace of God. I gave continual thanks and praise to him until, once more, God allowed us to slowly ascend up and out of that horrible place. *Thank-you God, for saving me and showing me the way. You are amazing and I love you with all that I am. I am yours.*

What was so amazing about that experience was the fact that I'd been in the dark pit of hell and escaped from it twice, several angels had told me that moment would come to pass a few years earlier. At the time I thought that I was being sent to hell, and with my mentality, I became frightened—I didn't know what I now know about abasement, conformity, and being in God's grace. I have since learned that our emotional and thoughtful perspectives can separate us from conformity with him when any form of doubt, fear, or disbelief is considered. The moral lesson for me was to learn how to be near God, and that I would need to understand and consistently remain humble and practice abasement with him. To remain close to him, I would continuously be in need of conforming to him in each moment, always.

Another interesting insight came to light as we returned from our visits to both places. I could see that upon my return my arms were raised slightly and bent at the elbows. It was just as I had seen my grandfathers arms raised at the moment he left this world. I was amazed to see the similarities and resemblance of my journey and his transitional experience from this life to the next.

Standing upright

Our next insightful moment transpired a few weeks later, on Thanksgiving evening, 2011. It was filled with incredible lessons of humility/abasement, celestial sights and insights and one of the greatest observations and perceptions of God. God had once again called upon me and instantly I was there. God then began to ask me questions, he searched my heart, and once more lowered me through abasement to be near him and to better understand the importance of the journey and of my past actions. I had a difficult time looking at God while he was calling me out, I started to blink, and God said stop blinking and stop turning your head away, look at me when I'm speaking. I realized God was unquestionably right and what I had done in my past was wrong, and while he continued speaking to me about what I and why I needed to listened, He began explaining what I needed to do for redemption. Jesus spoke on my behalf when God asked me questions I had difficulty answering, or when I was in need of help to properly explain my behavior to our Father. God described in great detail what was expected of me and how I was to live henceforth.

The beauty of the place I stood in was unparalleled; the magnificent rooms were enormous, I could see large tapestries and beautiful paintings hanging on many walls. The place I stood in was God's palace and each room appeared to connect to another room with even more beautiful furnishing and wondrous sights to it. Some of the ceilings decorated with chandeliers all soared upward and almost every room connected to another one. There were large open areas throughout his palace. I could see others moving about too, I could see some children were playing in other rooms; I saw many striking decorations and features inside each room.

God then commanded me to walk upright and straight, and I did. He told me many things about life and about my life, and he instantly took all the negative habits within my life and replaced them with good, virtuous, loving kindness. He told me who I am, where I am, what I am, and why I am. God changed me and began to teach me how to be a new man in true righteousness. God began by asking me the difference between abasement and transcendence. I said,

"Abasement with God is the lowering of oneself through a series of recognitions of one's past, which leads to humility, and which then leads to the exaltation of oneself by God. It's when lifted up by God that a true and gentle spiritual union can be formed."

"Transcendence with God is about how God— being God and above all things—travels and moves through all of existence. To transcend space, time, and beyond with God, one must first conform and learn to live as one with God."

The meeting lasted for what seemed like hours, and once God made sure that I was able to fully understand the importance of the lessons, we made our way back to the here and now. Soon thereafter I was on my bed once again, smelling the sweet fragrance of rose petals in the air.

I pray that you might know the true nature and grandeur of God Almighty, the Most High, the Alpha and the Omega, the supreme Spirit above all, whose perfect love will endure forever and ever.

I vanish

I had the ability to see all things within the moment—that it was now eleven thirty at night on Thanksgiving night, and that the classical radio station was rebroadcasting a superb symphony orchestra—and then I felt someone grab hold of both my arms. My remembrance of Gabriel's hold on me did not feel similar to the current one, so I looked around . . . and I saw God our father holding onto me. He had lifted me up slightly by my arms when it happened: the broadcaster of the Pittsburgh Symphony radio gave the introduction to the classical piece that was about to start, and he spoke reverently about love and of greatness. He spoke firmly of the brilliance of such phenomenal music, the compassion associated with the creation of it, and of God. Then he introduced Wolfgang Amadeus Mozart, and the Pittsburgh Symphony Orchestra slowly and eloquently began to play.

It was in that very moment, that very instant the commentary began, that I noticed my right hand begin to slowly disappear. This was different than when I had first visited heaven, I was physically being taken now. First my fingertips began to vanish, and that continued upward towards my body. My palms disappeared and I could see directly behind them as the background objects became visible, and then I began to pass completely out of sight. I didn't know what to expect; I only knew that God was taking me somewhere.

Some of the first sights were of the beyond yonder— the expanse and continuum in which all things God has created exist within. We were in a great abyss similar to what I had seen in several other occasions along this journey. We traveled for a brief period. There seemed to be a distinct haze everywhere, reminiscent to a dream, and it was here in this place where he showed me an object that appeared to be suspended in the great vastness, and as we traveled closer I could see it was a large piece of land shaped like an enormous cone with worldly features like green grass, dirt, and rocks. Beneath the surface was brown dirt, different rock formations, and everything else you would think of encountering underground. We slowly began to move around the suspended object while God helped me to understand that it was his creation in the beginning, before it became what it looks like now—before his creation of the world. We continued to move about the great vastness and encountered more of the same large land masses. They were all spread out from one another, all suspended in the great expanse. Some of them were similar in size while others were about five times as large as the first one. We moved in closer to one of the larger land masses, and I saw an enormous statue carved into the side of its lower section. As we passed by, I saw a person who paled in comparison to the size of the statue.

> *"Before the mountains were brought forth, or ever you had formed the earth and the world, from everlasting to everlasting you are God"* (PSALM 90:2).

Remaining quiet

We gradually moved from there into another area, where God instructed me to keep quiet. I was not sure at the time why, but I did not question him. We entered an extremely large stone building with vertically and horizontally flat symmetrical surfaces and walls. There were several walkways dividing specific places and areas within this place, and most of the areas inside of the dividing walkways were filled with deep water. I saw men and women covered entirely in both tan and white linen. They swam within that place with their clothes on, moving between sections. God told me it was how the people lived before boats existed; I later found out the ancient period was around 7000 BC.

It was at that point on our journey that Wolfgang Amadeus Mozart began to play, and his wonderful sounds accompanied our transcendent experience. God, as great as he is, wonderful in everything, continued moving us forward through his creations, through space and time.

The immense vastness and great continuum in which all things exist within was once more visible all around us. We were approaching another extremely large object that resembled an enormous rectangular screen with a slight glowing haze several feet thick all around the edges. From deep within that enormous object came a tiny centered image, and as it quickly moved closer toward us I could see that it was existence itself, while the large rectangular object held the parameters of reality. The image grew getting larger and larger until it completely filled the area we gazed upon, and then we'd entered into that moment somewhere back in time.

God's view places everything into perspective everywhere, always, and forever; the true magnitude of God's transcendence became completely evident and phenomenal.

The Roman era

At first I saw a man standing before me dressed in red garments and wearing sandals. Mountains stood in the near distance of that beautiful rugged place, and the ground was covered with sand and dirt. The sunshine warmed the air, and I felt its warmth on my arms and face. I experienced every sound and scent. Then I saw others moving about with this man, all of them fair-skinned and dressed in red garments, and all wearing leather sandals with cross straps tied up their legs. Because of their attire, I thought God, Jesus, and I must be in an ancient time, perhaps the Roman era. Many of the men were running, pushing, and shoving one another. They were all moving about hurriedly, seemingly for their lives, as they were forced into large wooden corrals. I remained silent though, despite my closeness to everyone there—I could have stretched out my arms and touched them; I could see the perspiration on their brows and the expressions on their faces.

Ancient eras

We transcended from era to era, and I would periodically think and express to God how beautiful and amazing the whole experience was. God would then remind me after each comment, to keep quiet during our journey. I still could not quite understand why. Instantly we would change locations to splendid far off places in the young and undeveloped world. We moved into the clouds and I could see snow packed along mountaintops. I could instantly feel the cold; but then God warmed me and we continued. I saw some type of structure and an entrance to someplace and then God told me we were at Olympus. We then entered an enormous structure and I saw the gods inside their temple. I even spoke the name Athena as I saw her sitting before us. We observed them for a brief moment. I could see they were all at least fifty feet tall and dressed in white robes or togas. They sat in large stone seats that were reminiscent of ancient Greece; the building had solid stone pillars inside and concrete and granite throughout.

Ancient Egypt

Next we visited a large stone structure, where six men were carving four great fifty-foot-tall statues along the side of a great wall. All of the men were dressed in white garments that were fashioned over their shoulders and hung low around their thighs. They all wore a belt or strap that went around their waists and shoulders and each of them had a very distinct looking hat covering their heads that fanned out behind their ears. From the carving of the statues and the way the men were dressed, I understood them all to be Egyptian. Then suddenly something inexplicable happened: I felt something inside of me and all my stomach muscles contracted, my inner being jolted, and suddenly the second statue from the left began to be affected and fell. As the head broke off from the wall and the upper body of the giant statue tumbled down, I heard the loud crash of stone slamming against other stone, and the men were barely able to move out of the way before it reached the ground. The statue had directly broken off from the wall and shattered into many pieces as it fell forward. I knew that I had been a part of something extraordinary. [God later told me that they felt what had happened in the temple. I didn't understand at the time but I would later find out the moment was documented as happening during the construction of the Abu Simbel temples of Ancient Egypt; they were constructed during the reign of Pharaoh Ramses II in the 13th century BC—over three thousand and seventy seven years ago.]

The great flood

God was showing me many of the greatest moments of existence firsthand. God, our father, the supreme Spirit, and Jesus Christ were taking me from the starting point of creation and leading me through epic moments in time. God showed me the great flood at the moment when the banks rose and the water overflowed, similar to another great flood I had a premonition of only weeks before. In my premonition, the water rose from the banks the same way the water before us did. Within a matter of seconds, the water swelled up and rolled over the banks to rush over all the landscape, and all while Wolfgang Amadeus Mozart's great music was contributing to each moment.

I continued seeing captivating events of people and places all over the world. God showed me life and how precious a gift it truly is and I could now see just how each moment led to the next, while each sight continuously revealed the paths and fates of people's existence. This was life as only God has allowed it to be.

Silence!

We continued to transcend throughout existence, and it was proving difficult to remain quiet. Perhaps it was the magnitude of the journey or perhaps it was the human mind's inability to grasp the magnitude of such a journey, but what is certain was my incapacity to refrain completely from thinking or speaking out loud. Once again I said aloud, "This is amazing." Instantly, God transcended us to a place near the mountain peaks and allowed me to feel the bitter cold climate. I gazed upon the snow packs on the cliffs and the hazy grey clouds lingering atop them. I was very cold, though, and my teeth began to chatter. God let me know it would help keep my mind from wondering and me from talking. After a few moments of enduring the climate, I quieted down and God removed the coldness. He let me know that if I could not refrain again from speaking out, he would put it right back. I thought about that for a moment and asked God if he could go ahead and let me shiver for a while because I did not think I would be able to stop right away, and he did. He put the cold right back onto me, and so I shivered for a little while longer. Sure enough, after I shivered and kept quiet for a while God removed the bitter cold as we continued moving forward once again.

Life is abundant and each moment is so very fragile.

Being heard

Having been warmed up by God, we moved into another scenic place. We passed through the branches and leaves of several trees, and when we cleared them I could see the slopes of the mountains surrounding us and the valley below. I could see the lush greenery of the grass and the rockiness of the terrain as we flew downward toward the base of the mountains. Our pace was moderately slow, and the classical music of Wolfgang Amadeus Mozart was still being played by the Pittsburgh Symphony Orchestra. *Thank-you, God, for such a wonderful journey, you are amazing.*

Down in the valley was a wonderfully large dwelling of sorts; I thought perhaps it was a city. It reminded me of early Jerusalem. Its walls were very tall and built up as if to keep others out. We continued to move to the next locations. When we entered the next place, I saw several people gathered together for some unknown reason. I hadn't quite noticed yet that although we were actually moving through space and time, we were not visible, yet we were completely within each moment. The very moment I observed that was when I had the next verbal outburst. Just then I spoke out loud and one of those gathering looked in our direction. The person nearest us clearly heard me and turned toward us. I saw his facial expression, and his reaction indicated he was not sure what he was looking at. Then he said,

"What is that?" before calling out to someone else nearby to come quickly and see what he was looking at.

We left instantly, and I began to better understand how my verbosity might affect things.

Fragile moments

From these wondrous experiences I could see that life exists on so many levels and our past and our future are alive, and they are just as delicate and fragile as we are. Every moment we live through—whether in the past, present, or future—is tremendous and completely sensitive and vital to our very existence. We must be mindful of every thought, every action, and everything we do within this world and beyond; it all matters and impacts each of our lives significantly. The interwoven complexities and intricacies of our lives cross the boundaries of space and time every moment our mind remembers the past or accurately predicts the future. Although these occurrences typically conclude with a brief realization or emotion, I believe it's that fractional instance of remembrance (or of predictability) that allows us to experience a momentary connection to the moment in question (through transcendence). This adds in our ability to live in the reality of the present.

Our travels included many far off destinations and locations of places and events that preceded recorded history and when we had reached the end of our transcendent journey through many of the greatest moments of creation, I said to God,

"That was an absolutely amazing journey, thank-you for sharing this with me." Then I thought about the Ark of the Covenant and asked God about it.

God then asked me, "Would you like to see it?"

I replied, "No, I'll see it at another time; the journey has been perfect."

We began to transcend through space and time once again when I heard a bold voice in the background—the bold voice belonged to the same man who spoke reverently about the greatness of creation and its passion at the beginning of our journey. He spoke of God and once more introduced Wolfgang Amadeus Mozart, and the Pittsburgh Symphony Orchestra movingly began to play once again. God had brought us back to the beginning of our journey to our first locations through time. As the orchestra played and the feeling of complete joy and happiness engulfed me, I was completely captivated with the greatness of God. I could see amazing clouds and a distinct glow and then I noticed we were exiting the moment into the great continuum in which all things exist. We passed through the parameters of reality, through the large rectangular shape and into the beyond yonder. Again, we began to transcend space and time. I had a weightless feeling of peacefulness come over me, like I was flying, and I could see God and Jesus flying right alongside me. I seemed to fly as gracefully as they did, and it looked like they were having as much fun as I was. I thought lovingly about them, noticing they are how they are, and I began to fly towards them both, and as I reached them, God our father, grabbed a hold of me and spun us in a circle and thrust me forward towards infinity. I flew with my arms falling behind me and my cheeks rippling because of how fast I was moving, I then rolled up like a ball, rolling down a hill towards everywhere and nowhere extremely fast, completely filled with joy, laughing, and smiling. *Thank-you, God, for allowing that incredible moment for me, as you have allowed every moment to be incredible since before the beginning of creation.*

The why

I could see now that when I had spoken out loud that it was a seemingly unplanned and triggered response of awe. And God was about to reveal to me why I could not yet stop the outburst, why I could not listen, why I could not yet get his simple request straight.

As we entered the next moment I could see we had moved into a heavenly structure made of a clear type of crystal. The walls were somewhat transparent and there were fifty-foot-tall ceilings throughout, sometimes even higher. I would later learn it was God's crystal palace we were moving through. The same shiny palace I had seen several times before. The floors were sparkling and shimmery, and sometimes the rooms had large water features within them. The grand fountains throughout God's shiny palace reminded me of the large fountains of many cities of Europe. Everything was enormous, with very distinct grandeur and illumination. The structure was quite unique and within each room of this incredible place was even more beauty than the room before. I was taken in with just how much every specific spot was designed wonderfully.

I would periodically speak out loud into the room—for some unknown reason—something selfish, or at other times something that seemed inappropriate. I tried to keep the whole journey in perspective and remain focused within each moment, but then I expressed how impatient

I was within specific areas. God told me to be quiet, and I tried to remain focused and stay quiet, but I found that soon thereafter I would say something else. I knew it was the overall experience of the journey that was causing these outbursts, and I was acting childish, feeling overwhelmed with the inability to stop.

God then guided us into another grand room, where I was introduced to a man I was told was the first one who had transcended into heaven to also find God. He had done so many years before, back when men still used horses as their main mode of transportation. Initially I was a bit surprised with his appearance and how different he looked, and my greeting felt inept. I was startled as I was introduced to him. His cheeks were covered in what looked like red paint and He sat dining at a table (in God's crystal palace) filled with many different dishes before him. I thought my behavior was offensive to him until he replied to me in the same way as I addressed him. Then I thought the first meeting with him was okay, because I heard him tell God he liked me. I didn't quite know how to respond to him properly; there were many strange feelings moving within me and I was stumbling in my efforts to come across well-mannered.

We then moved into another large area where there were twenty-four elders, male and female, dressed in white robes and speaking confidently. God emphasized the importance of the moment and asked me to listen to them as they spoke. The room was extensive and had a domed cathedral ceiling. I could see wood paneling along the walls. The elders spoke of history and events I had been a part of. They spoke of how special an experience this was and what it would mean to the world. They spoke of truth and of the importance of the message. I tried to listen as they continued to speak of the deliverance. I thought again of having transcended space and time with God, and now I was in a place where I was truly beginning to fathom the moment, truly beginning to see the grandeur of my epic journey of abasement and true spirituality and conformity with God, when suddenly I did it again. I spoke out loud about how impatient I had become. Once more, God asked me to be quiet and to listen. I did my best but still I found I could not, suddenly and again I thought about their subject matter and I found myself moving towards them all. As I moved across the middle of the room, past all twenty-four elders deep in discussion, I once again spoke out. God could see that I was in need of his help and of patience; he grabbed hold of me just before I reached them all and helped me to calm down. At the time I was having some difficulty with understanding the importance of this encounter and what this would mean for everyone.

I could not yet grasp the ability to stop behaving in that way, but then God allowed me to see the truth about him and his righteousness:

> *God is unchanging; he is constant and*
> *unwavering in all that he does.*

God's lesson that he had been teaching me was to be unwavering, just as he is, within any moment, and to not quickly react to any circumstance that arises. I could then see that if I was to respond the same way God does towards all that he encounters, then I would share and experience each moment of love, because every moment with God is love. He could instantly feel when I had been hesitant or acting timidly towards a lesson, and I was unable to learn the lesson of patience until God truly showed me how to live in righteousness.

He cares

When God revealed the lesson that showed me how to live without a sense of guilt, as if I had not committed sin, he expressed to me how special that moment truly was. He pointed out that although I had some difficulty understanding a few of the lessons he taught me, I did not quit or give up. He told me how special I was and instantly filled me with the confidence I was lacking while timid. Our Father and our Lord believed in me! I realized at that point that with my past behavior and the way I had treated people, there was really no person who still believed in me. I began to cry. I realized that my life had been consumed with self and selfishness, and that even while God had shown me sights from the beginning of creation to his miraculous crystal palace, I was still behaving in a childish way. I thought about what he had shown me, each lesson of abasement, and each lesson that was compounding into another. That part seemed to be one of the most important of all the lessons. When God told me of how he believed in me, he blessed me and graced me with confidence. That confidence helped to renew and reestablish the surety of God's blessing. I was truly standing upright, without condemnation, as the tears ceased and God's righteousness broke through.

Confidence

The hesitance and fearfulness that had once been visible within certain parts of the journey was now gone. I awoke to righteousness, and upon awakening I could see everything within the crystal palace even more perfectly—shining and sparkling upper levels, and other people going about their blessed lives. I felt as if I had a new emotional and thoughtful perspective, and I felt empowered and sensational inside—strong and assured of everything.

I began to boldly speak to God about how wonderful I felt and how everything had changed within. I heard Jesus speaking to God about what was happening. Then I realized I had been so enveloped in conversation with God, I had not even noticed we had changed locations. We were now in the very first place I had transcended to a year earlier, when I had first experienced conformity with God, where we had first met in an abasing party.

God also told me that he was now going to lead us through the next moments. I had not realized that with the boldness and confidence God had graced me with; I had been briefly leading our way to and through several moments. I no longer felt inferior in any way while in his presence. God gave me the experience in order to build a greater understanding of the true limitless abilities that are within each of our lives, *all thanks to God.*

The waters of life

Next thing I knew, I was kneeling before God's throne and then I remembered I had been there before the last time I was in heaven. The grand throne room had a radiant white glow all throughout, similar to clouds, and God's throne was gold with meticulous features inlaid within its design. With emanating love, God spoke with me from his throne of who I am and how incredible the journey was. He sanctified me in his words reminding me of who I had become in his righteousness and of how our wonderful journey had brought me there. He shared with me how incredible everything always is in righteousness. He showed me who I am and reminded me again he had created me.

I could now see that all the shining sparkles throughout each room came from this very spot, from God, and they began there in the throne room. The glimmers and sparkles of light reminded me of how sunlight sparkles on water, and I realized I was witnessing the waters of life flowing throughout God's amazing crystal palace and into existence itself. After our meeting concluded and God bestowed upon me his amazing blessing, he led us through another huge crystal room, then through a couple of double doors, and into an outdoor area just outside the palace, where everything was also shimmering and sparkling. I could see a large water fountain and an even larger body of water nearby which looked like a crystal pool, sparkling and shimmering.

God asks again

God asked me again what my opinion was of the Bible. I thought about the question very carefully. Remembering how I had answered the first time God had asked that question of me, I truly knew now of the great importance of learning the Word of God, and when I had first begun my journey I had little understanding. Now I could see the truth. I had a greater amount of understanding, a greater amount of knowledge, and a greater amount of wisdom. I said,

"I think it's amazing and well-written, and I think it helps all people find their way to you, God," and then I said, "There were some parts I wish had a deeper explanation of spirituality and living in abasement with you."

I hoped that the comment was not offensive or disrespectful in any way towards Jesus, and I mentioned that to him as we continued speaking. We talked some more about abasement and spirituality, concluding with my asking both God and Jesus again to let me write of my understandings and experiences for those in need of a deeper level of spiritual discernment. That was precisely what God had asked of me in the beginning of my journey, during the journey, and now at his palace concluding our journey.

I felt complete serenity; I had an amazing sense of peacefulness. I could feel the wisdom God had bestowed upon me. I had learned so many incredible truths, and I knew that each lesson, each sight, each part of his blessings are all miracles that he has allowed for. *Thank-you, God, with all my heart; thank-you.*

Readjusting to the present

When the journey through space, time and heaven had concluded I slowly floated back down onto my bed and everything within my room came back into view. I felt especially calm, at complete peace. The first thing I heard was the voice of someone saying,

"He's back." I could see the many spirits, angels, and others all gathered together in my room. I saw the spiritual image of a man sitting in the lotus position and floating, he had a brilliant glowing aura all around him. I knew he too had transcended to that very moment to witness the moment I returned, and once again, I heard the radio presenter introduce Mozart and play the same classical piece that I had heard several times throughout our journey. Now it was beginning all over again, just as if it had begun to play the very first time. When I checked the time, it was still eleven thirty at night. God and I had just transcended to the beginning of creation, before time ever existed, then throughout the centuries, then into heaven and throughout all of God's crystal palace, and then back into the present; all just before the exact time we first left. God told me he would stay with me and help me to adjust to the present once again, and that because of my experiences I was going to have to learn to move slowly and be patient. I asked God how long we were gone for, and God told me two and-a-half months, but that it seemed more like two-and-a-half minutes.

I thought for God, transcendence must be like taking a walk—simply refreshing—but for me, it would take me a few days to readjust to the present. [God said I could do it by maintaining my composure when specific occurrences happened. He spoke of maintaining focus and clarity onto him, and in order to do that I would need to remain focused on abasing conversations and conforming thoughts of him, to him, and with him.] I sat on my bed and felt the power of the Lord everywhere, and my first thought was of peacefulness and of hope for my family to find peace. I began to pray for my parents, for my brother and his family, for my children, for my aunts and uncles, for my cousins, and everyone, everywhere whom I loved, and for all those who had been having difficulty finding peace in their lives. I asked God to help them all come together and get through and over their differences with one another and anyone else, and for them all to find the peace they were lacking. I thought that was the perfect way to start— at home with baby steps. I have always believed you have to crawl before you can walk, walk before you can run, and run before you can fly. These baby steps and prayer were just the beginning.

Surviving transcendence

I began to focus on abasement and being in abasement with God. I could clearly see that my ability to speak loudly had been hindered, because when I tried to pray aloud each word was a whisper. God speaks to all of us in the same way, righteously and in a whisper. God told me that the behavior of my past was now over and that I was to walk straight and upright, he asked me to be abstinent in every way, and so I become celibate, so that I could clearly

273

see the truth of relationships. I was to focus on all that is good, true, pure, loving, and kind.

God's new information began to fill my heart with emotions and my mind with a great deal of thoughts and when it first started, I could feel my entire body start to shiver and my heartbeat rapidly increase. That was when God told me to focus onto him and remain calm or the effects could lead to a possible occurrence of sudden transcendence. After a couple of those readjusting moments, God helped me by taking it from me, enduring the phenomenon for me, and then giving the ability back when the strong trembling and difficult part had subsided. He continued to teach me how to do that for myself.

I stayed focused by whispering to God.

"God you are amazing and wonderful; thank-you for helping me to be here and to be close to you.

"You are wonderful in every moment.

"Thank-you.

"Bless you."

That allowed the aftereffects of transcendence on my mind, body, and spirit to slowly fade until I was once again calm and our spiritual union was strengthened. I thought about those effects for a while and thought that they must be due to the combining of reality of the here and now with the comprehension of transcendence of space and time. I asked God,

"How is it that I was able to move through space and time without causing injury to my body or to myself? How did I survive the journey?"

He told me that he had done something specific to my body that allowed for it to occur. Immediately I recognized what he was referring to—he had put some sort of unique, godly mist onto my body. I had experienced that same type of mist before when I first burst into tiny particles of energy—the same form of mist which came down from a large tube-like object upon all those who stood upon a platform, allowing them to then travel after bursting into tiny particles of energy. It was the same mist that I had inhaled and tasted while on that platform. That mist protected me while I traveled in the same way as the angels, and same way as God, and Jesus.

And on it goes

I was beginning to understand the adaptation process when I then heard someone asking about abasement with God. Instantly we seemed to be somewhere else in the world, and as I looked upon this person, I heard God ask me if I was going to answer them. I could see we had moved into the place where the person asking was at. I answered this persons question about abasement, but I had to stop and think when I found another of his questions difficult to understand. I then asked this person to be patient for a moment, I thought about the question asked, and then I asked God, who told me to ask Jesus; then I asked Jesus, and then Jesus shared the answer and then I responded to the question. God then allowed us to move forward in our spiritual union. I could see it was there in spiritual union with God, where he helped me to understand how I should be, what I should say, or what I shouldn't say. The conversation lasted for several minutes, and then suddenly it happened again: I heard another person asking of what abasement with God is and instantly I found myself before her speaking with her about how abasement with God transpires, what it looks like, and how to enter into a spiritual union with him. Again, I found that I would speak carefully and truthfully of abasement with the person asking the questions, while God and Jesus continued to reveal to me what to say and how to be within those moments. I could see that because I had abasement in my heart and was focused on being in abasement with God, anytime it was referenced in the world we instantly transcended to some place to be in the direct presence of those who were in need of the answer.

Our wonderful conversations on abasement lasted for several more hours, as we transcended from place to place throughout the world then finally readjusting to the present, while God and Jesus stayed right there by my side, guiding me through each wonderful moment. I felt complete in every way as we continued sharing in laughter, truths, hopes, stories of the past and of the future, and while having conversations of transcendence and spiritual unions of abasement. I felt humbled in knowing the entire journey happened because God had allowed it to, knowing that our gentle and true spiritual unions and our abasing moments led to conformity, and that we can and have been asked to learn to live as one with God.

A special walk

Early next morning, God and I still joined in gentle union, traveled to another place unlike any I'd ever seen before. We instantly moved to a large city in heaven where he showed me around many beautiful places. As God and I walked and spoke of our journey, he expressed how he was glad that I was finally there with him in that moment. He mentioned he had been waiting for a long time for us to experience what we had just done. He spoke with me about my parents, describing how they too would become spiritual, and when he told me this, I had the same reaction as while in the temple in ancient Egypt. From deep within, my whole body jolted once again. God then told me about the earth moving and the statue falling during the construction of the temple. I didn't quite understand at the time what temple he was referring to. Then he began to share with me what he had planned for me, and what I would be apart of in the future. As he began sharing the moments that would come to pass in my life, I realized I was at complete peace with God, and while in spiritual union together we had accomplished everything in a very special way.

The upper level of heaven

We spoke for a while longer about transcendence and then instantly we transcended into another part of heaven greater than every other place we had seen before. We entered a radiant and majestic place with multiple levels on top of one another, all surrounding an oval shaped section that opened up and allowed for each level and each oval shaped entrance to be visible. As I gazed into each oval section, it revealed the home of God and his family. I saw many sections evenly spaced from one another encompassing the entire structure, and on every level, there were many observances of deity. Each regal place lit with an amazing luminance, reminding me of how remarkable a journey this truly was. As we moved around that incredible location, I saw many other sections all opened up and all with more deity dressed in long white robes and living graciously.

As we approached another magnificent area, I could see open platforms with circular steps and multiple levels. There were many deities visibly working on incredible tasks. This level of heaven was what I believed it to look like. Never before could I have imagined such a place would have existed, had I not been there to see it for myself. I saw many of those who were working and living there, each of them with eloquence and grace and once again I was standing before God the father and the supreme spirit.

God mention my prayers from several days earlier and how he enjoyed hearing them, and how he was glad that I had made the journey. In my prayers, I had been praying for the ability to put an end to the causality of all human suffering. It was delightful to hear God mention that prayer. God then introduced me to those closest to him. He stood before me, and as we faced each other he left me with a strong piece of advice.

God said, "Do not be timid."

As we moved through that magical place and into one of the oval shaped sections and into another room, God instructed me to lie down and rest myself while he conversed with another. As I relaxed, he told me to keep quiet and listen, then began to speak with deity about what we had just accomplished together. It was incredible to hear God speak in detail of each moment we had experienced. He spoke of the exact instance we left, he spoke of Mozart's famed music, and then as I heard something else that intrigued me, I tried to speak up. God asked me again to listen. Instantly I felt the center of my lips button together. Immediately I got the point, and I quieted down. Then I heard God speaking of another part of the journey that once again intrigued me, and I managed to unbutton my lip, and I tried to speak out, only this time I had the feeling of not having a tongue. God was keeping me from speaking in a unique way. Hearing God speak was phenomenal, and I simply felt like sharing in the conversation and expressing how brilliant I thought the journey was. God shared the entire story, and then the one God spoke with asked me what I thought of all we had done. The glorious experience had not fully registered yet. I expressed my thoughts about the whole experience. Looking back I realize the grace and magnitude of such an insightful and Godly revelation allowed for a wonderful view of his magnificent creation, and as we crossed through space, time and the throughout the heavens, I realized how utterly brilliant, and perfectly God the journey truly was.

Everything's okay

When the conversations concluded, and we transcended back home, I spoke with God about how every moment with him made me feel. I began to contemplate the beginning and every incredible sight and sound of the journey we had just taken. There was music playing in the background, and once more the spiritual union we had formed showed how God began speaking directly to me using the lyrics of the music. This time as Coldplay sang and performed the song "The Scientist" I could see it fit, similarly describing the journey. I had just gone up to heaven to meet with him, and he had just taken us back to the start of creation. Thinking to God again about how marvelous he is in everything, I knew he had put that song and the moment together just for this realization. I began to understand how incredible every moment of life with God truly is. As I slowly drifted off into a peaceful and deep sleep knowing everything would be okay, I instantly knew that it always was.

The Beginning...

To the Reader

Understanding that all that has ever been done in the history of existence has been done because God has allowed for it, and he has allowed me to share these truths with you. Each lesson and experience brought forth from God, our father, Jesus, Lord and Savior, and the Holy Spirit.

With the love of God, our father and Jesus, Lord and Savior, I give thanks and praise in the spirit of faith that you may each be mindful of the knowledge of the divine journey. I pray that you may continue to rest in God's grace, doing all things for one another without expectations and without complaint, with kindness and gentleness, in the spirit of love. I pray for you constantly that you keep the Word of God in the forefront of your life as you do what's right in his sight; that you exercise self-control with integrity, honesty, patience; and that you live honorably and morally in faith and righteousness.

I hope with all that I am that the good and true life that you live will bring you closer to a spiritual union with God, that with humility/abasement and conformity with him you may truly learn what it means to live as one with God, and that the journey and these miraculous events will help comfort you through knowing that each of our lives has purpose and meaning above, below, and beyond.

This wonderful experience concludes the way it began, with God everywhere and in everything, always and forever. I now understand that God allows me to feel complete in knowing him, being in his presence, and having seen him directly. I now have the greatest sense of peace, happiness, and contentment knowing **he is in every moment with us all, and is always watching over us.**